SCANDINAVIA

DENMARK, FINLAND, ICELAND, NORWAY AND SWEDEN

Welcome to Scandinavia

Sylvie Nickels

Collins
Glasgow and London

Cover photograph
Zefa: Lofotenhavn

Photographs
J. Allan Cash Ltd.
pp. 40 (l.), 47 (inset), 61, 62, 64, 69, 72 (bkgrd and inset: top l.), 88 (l.),
90, 94, 95, 96, 102 (l., rt), 104, 107, 113 (inset), 116 (btm), 121 (top), 123

Danish Tourist Board
pp. 35 (btm), 36, 48, 49, 50, 51, 52

Solarfilma, Iceland
p. 72 (inset: rt)

Van Phillips
pp. 35 (top), 39, 40 (rt), 41, 46–7 (bkgrd), 82 (inset: top l., rt), 97

Photobank
pp. 77, 78, 86 (rt), 88 (rt), 103, 116 (top), 117 (top)

Picturepoint Ltd.
pp. 58 (bkgrd), 59, 60, 67, 72 (inset: btm l.), 76, 82 (bkgrd and inset: btm l.),
86 (l.), 87, 105, 106, 113 (bkgrd), 120, 121 (btm), 122

Swedish Tourist Board
pp. 109, 117 (btm)

Town Plans
M. and R. Piggott

Illustrations
pp. 6–7 Peter Joyce

Regional Maps
Mike Shand, Iain Gerard

First published 1983
Revised edition published 1987
Copyright © text: Sylvie Nickels 1983
Copyright © maps: Wm. Collins, Sons & Co. Ltd.
Published by William Collins Sons and Company Limited
Printed in Great Britain

ISBN 0 00 447527 5

HOW TO USE THIS BOOK

The contents page of this book shows how the countries are divided up into tourist
regions. The book is in two main sections: general information and gazetteer. The
latter is arranged in the tourist regions with an introduction and a regional map
(detail below left). There are also plans of main cities (detail below right). All
main entries listed in the gazetteer are shown on the regional maps. Places
to visit and leisure facilities available in each region and city are indicated
by symbols. Main roads, railways and airports are shown on the maps.

Regional Maps

Town Plans

	Regional Maps				Town Plans
	Museum/gallery		Zoo		Museum/gallery
	Religious building	m	Ancient monument	✝	Religious building
	Main airport	♣	Park		Castle/fortress
	Other airport	🐦	Bird life		Interesting building
	Castle/fortress		Mines/caves		Theatre
	Climbing/mountainous		Walking/hiking		Library
	Interesting building		Water sports		Town hall
	Boating/sailing		Canoeing	⊠	Post office
	Gardens			*i*	Information
	Amusement park			POL	Police
	Skiing/winter sports			♣	Park
					Garden
					Railway station
					Bus terminal
				ⓟ	Car park

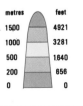

metres	feet
1500	4921
1000	3281
500	1640
200	656
0	0

———— motorway
= = = = motorway under
construction
———— other roads
———— railway

CONTENTS

Regions
Denmark

Finland

Norway

Sweden

SCANDINAVIA

If there is one commodity that Scandinavia has more than most holiday regions it is space: an infinity caught between mountains, forests, lakes, fjords or rolling sand dunes. The statistics speak for themselves. The combined areas of Denmark, Finland, Iceland, Norway and Sweden (nearly 1,300,000sq km/500,000sq mi) would swallow up the UK comfortably five times over or cover most of Alaska; yet the total population of around 20 million is less than those of London and New York put together. And to go with all that space are the amenities which the sun-worshipping Nordic nations make the best possible use of during their short but often brilliant summers.

From the south of Denmark at latitude 55°N to Norway's North Cape at latitude 71°N, this enormous area embraces a great variety of terrain and climate. Much of Denmark, moulded by good husbandry, has the homely quality of the English countryside, and weather patterns are similar too. Western Norway's dramatic, tortuous fjords bite deep into the mountainous spine that forms much of the border with neighbouring Sweden. From it, the rivers pour down through the Swedish valleys that range from the grandiose to the gently mellow to reach the Gulf of Bothnia and the Baltic Sea via tens of thousands of lakes and a vast acreage of forest or farmland. Finland is more of the same, relatively low lying so that its huge horizons seem to add an extra dimension, interrupted by parallel ridges left by the last Ice Age. The north of Scandinavia is rather loosely referred to as Lapland – that area of northern Norway, Sweden and Finland where a few tens of thousands of the Lapps, or Same people, live in lonely landscapes characterized by bare-topped fells, sparse forests and rolling tundra north of the Arctic Circle. It is a region where the sun shines 24 hours a day for up to six weeks around midsummer, depending on latitude, matched by a similar period around midwinter when it does not shine at all. Yet winter nights rarely have the velvet darkness of more southern latitudes, for the sky flares for hours with colour from the invisible sun, the snow adds an eerie luminosity, and on the coldest clearest nights the aurora borealis (northern lights) sends magic veils rippling silently above the land. Finally, far out to sea, Iceland sits astride the Mid-Atlantic Ridge, that massive fault in the earth's crust which created volcanic landscapes that contrast with the vivid green of coastal valleys.

Administratively, each country is divided into counties or provinces, sub-divided into communes (local districts or municipalities). Scandinavia's brand of democracy has resulted in a proliferation of political parties that makes for rather frequent changes of government (eg Finland has 9 parties, Denmark 10), often necessitating coalitions, but the trend has long been a liberal form of social democracy with a few experimental interruptions. The Scandinavian passion for freedom is matched by a deep sense of justice. It is significant that the post of Ombudsman, who investigates complaints against the actions of government departments, originated here (as early as 1809 in Sweden). There is also a refreshing absence of class divisions even though an impressive range of noble titles survives, especially in Sweden. Denmark, Norway and Sweden each has a constitutional monarchy (the Danes' is the oldest in Europe). Finland and Iceland are headed by Presidents appointed for several years. Indeed, Iceland has the world's first freely elected woman head of state, Vigdís Finnbogadóttir. In all five countries, social welfare is of a high order – Sweden has one of the most advanced systems of social care anywhere in the world.

Though inter-Nordic cooperation binds the five countries closely together, the relationship of each with the rest of the world is very individual. Denmark is the only one to belong to the European Economic Community, though the others are all associated with the European Free Trade Association and have important trade links with the EEC. Denmark, Iceland and Norway are members of NATO, while Sweden and Finland are neutral, the latter insisting on an unequivocal policy of neutrality to maintain its finely balanced position between east and west. All these peace-loving nations have contributed major efforts to reduce the tensions of our troubled world; all the more shattering therefore, was the violent murder of the Swedish Prime Minister Olof Palme, early in 1986. As far as religion is concerned,

e Lutheran Church is dominant in
ll five countries, though several Free
hurches thrive in Sweden, while Finland
as a substantial minority following the
rthodox faith.

Throughout Scandinavia, the standard
living is very high indeed. Increased
echanization and diversification in recent
cades have modified dependence on the
aditional occupations of agriculture in
enmark, fishing in Iceland, fishing,
rming and forestry in Norway, the forest
dustries of Finland, and timber and iron
e in Sweden; but these are still very im-
ortant. Other specialities have emerged.
or example, forming the back-bone of the
anish economy are innumerable small
terprises. Sweden has moved into ad-
anced technology, especially machinery
d electrical equipment, and its achieve-
ents in worker participation, notably in
e car industry, are well known. Norway's
orth Sea oil riches have revolutionized
onomic life. Finland has made huge
rides in the metal working industry
nce World War II. Iceland is currently
arnessing and marketing some of the
calculable energy bottled up under-
round and in its thunderous waterways.
candinavian know-how is a major in-
sible export, which extends to setting
p paper mills in developing African
untries or building luxury hotels by East
urope's Black Sea beaches. In manu-
cturing, a whole range of first-class
oducts have emerged on to the world's
arkets, from Swedish cut glass and in-
pensive furniture, Finnish fashions,
anish silver and porcelain to Norwegian
nitwear.

A genuine interest in and flair for good
sign is common to all the Nordic peoples.
he 'average' Dane, Finn, Icelander,
orwegian, Swede, really cares – and
nows – who has designed the cut glass
owl, stainless steel cutlery, cups and
ucers or the lampstand in daily use.
hey also prefer to embellish their walls
ith original paintings rather than repro-
ctions, and are voracious readers of

their own and the world's literature.

The toughness of much of Scandinavia's
terrain and the rigorous climate for much
of the year moulded the pioneer spirit
which resulted in the remarkable adventures of early Scandinavian history,
outlined in the next section. Similarly
it has produced some of the world's
greatest latter-day explorers such as
Amundsen, Nansen, Nordenskiöld and
Rasmussen. Scandinavians share a splendidly dry sense of humour and the ability
to laugh at themselves. But there are many
differences, too. The Danes are the ex-
troverts of northern Europe, the most
relaxed, the easiest to meet and know. The
Norwegians and Finns are much more
reserved, offering endless help if asked,
although they themselves are rather self-
sufficient. The Finns especially tend to
a contemplativeness that can at times
amount to the morose. The Swedes, tem-
peramentally in the middle, are given
to sensitivity over their material wealth
and their neutrality. Language problems
are minimal, however, as English is
spoken to an extent that often puts to
shame those who speak only their mother
tongue.

Compared with more southerly parts of
Europe, sights of historic or architectural
interest, though many and varied, are
not so thickly concentrated away from
main cities and, except in Denmark,
distances between can be considerable.
This fact, allied to the beauty of the
natural surroundings almost everywhere,
makes the whole region particularly well
suited to two types of holiday: those devoted to outdoor activities, and touring
on a modest or grand scale by car or by
public transport. Enjoy Yourself (p. 22)
outlines the many facilities available
for special interests, but to those must be
added the sheer joy of magnificent scenery.
You will soon notice, too, that the tendency for most Scandinavians to escape
from their well-organized cities into the
surrounding countryside at every opportunity is more than just the answer to an
aesthetic need. It is also the need to feel
part of nature, whether it is picking
mushrooms in the woods, messing about
in a boat, hewing wood or drawing water,
or testing wits or stamina against some
natural element.

For the purposes of touring and easy
reference, each country has been divided
according to size or topography as follows. **Denmark** falls naturally into two
main sections: Jylland (Jutland), Fyn
(Funen), Langeland and Aerø; Sjælland
(Sealand) – which includes Copenhagen –
Møn, Falster and Lolland; with short sum-
maries for Bornholm and the Faroes.

(Greenland, though part of the Danish Realm, is so far away and sparsely populated that it is outside the scope of this guide.) **Finland** is split into the South covering most of the lake districts and archipelagoes; the North from Oulu through Lappi (Finnish Lapland) to its northernmost boundaries. **Iceland** is treated as one region (subdivided into North and South) because of the many possibilities for round trips. **Norway** has three sections: Eastern Norway, including Oslo and the eastern valleys; the Western Fjords covering Bergen and the famous fjord country; North Norway from Trondheim to the Soviet border, including Finnmark (Norwegian Lapland) and the North Cape. **Sweden** also comprises three sections: South Sweden including Gothenburg and all the southern provinces across to the island of Gotland; Central Sweden with Stockholm and the folkloric provinces of Dalarna and Värmland; North Sweden including most of the high mountains and Lapland up to the borders with Norway and Finland.

Though the freedom of your own four wheels has obvious advantages, the excellent public transport services outlined in Internal Travel (p. 14), and various organized tours of excursions out of main resorts, make it possible to see a great deal at reasonable cost. Magnificent scenery abounds and the subtle quality of changing light is matchless in more southerly latitudes. That is completely free.

THE PAST

Archaeological finds indicate that from a time following the retreat of the ice in the last glacial period, early man has moved over the more habitable parts of Scandinavia, food gathering, hunting and fishing. By about 1500 BC, during the Bronze Age, a people of Germanic origin occupied Denmark and southern parts of the Scandinavian peninsula where they developed a culture of villages, land cultivation, religious ritual and a high skill in craftsmanship. Numerous rock carvings date from this period. With the Iron Age and the northward extension of Roman boundaries, Scandinavia first enters written history. The Emperors Augustus and Nero sent fleets into northern waters and Pliny the Elder, Tacitus and the geographer Ptolemy were writing of what had been seen. We are even given a glimpse of some strange tribes, the Lapps and Finns living far to the north or east of the Germanic tribes of the Scandinavian peninsula.

At the beginning of the Viking era, Scandinavia had little political entity, consisting only of many provinces sharing a more or less common language. Though only loosely linked, the energetic people of these northern territories were soon to make their fearful and forceful mark on European history. By the middle of the 8th century, their shipwrights had developed sailing craft to a remarkable standard: high-prowed long ships, fine examples of which are preserved in the museums at Roskilde, Oslo and elsewhere. It was not as farmers or traders that the Vikings were to be first known but as raiders and robbers. Impelled by over-population in a harsh land, and no doubt also by a spirit of adventure, they roamed far across Europe for most of the 9th and 10th centuries. They made swift pirate raids at first; later, massive assaults resulted in colonizing as well as conquering. They settled in much of western Europe, including Britain and Normandy, occupied Iceland and Greenland, and even discovered North America.

It was during this time that some sort of political order was formed out of earlier disarray, and organized states emerged with well-defined boundaries ruled by monarchs with such splendid names as Erik Bloodaxe and Harald Fairhair. Denmark, under its rulers Gorm the Old, Harald Bluetooth and Svein Forkbeard became a powerful kingdom in the 10th century; it was Harald (950–986) who brought Christianity to Denmark, and Norway under the political control of the Danish crown. The greatest of Danish Kings was Knut (Canute), king of England as well as Denmark and Norway. But Knut's over-large North Sea empire collapsed on his death when political control was reversed and Denmark now became subject to the Norwegian king Magnus the Good, until 1046. In 1064, Svein Estridsson became king of Denmark and, following many years of war with Norway, his country settled down within what were to be her boundaries for many years (for a long time they included what is today southern Sweden).

It was in this period that the first towns were founded in Denmark, the first bishoprics created and a substantial series of fortifications were constructed, including part of the Danevirke, intended to secure Jutland's southern border against Charlemagne. The Viking Age in Sweden followed a rather different course; their efforts were directed south and east rather than west, and they travelled as traders as well as raiders. Sailing Russia's great rivers they reached both Byzantium and the Caspian Sea. The Slav name for Viking was Rus – hence the name Russia.

Christianity came more slowly to Sweden, and not without resistance and bloodshed. It was well into the 12th century before it really gained a firm hold and an archbishopric was established at Uppsala. And it was Christian crusading zeal, as well as territorial greed, that brought heathen Finland under Swedish domination. Ethnically and linguistically unrelated to the Scandinavian family, the Finns are believed to have arrived from somewhere east of the Volga at about the beginning of the Christian era. Erik IX, Sweden's patron saint, moved into Finland in 1157 and, with him, helping to lead the Christian mission, was the Englishman Bishop Henry, soon to be slaughtered for his pains. Thus Christianity's first martyr in Finland became her patron saint.

Following the Viking period, the Scandinavian countries began to concentrate on their own resources and trade; timber, iron and fish products were important exports as they are now. So profitable became this trade that the Hanseatic League of north German cities cast covetous eyes upon it, and as a result much commercial independence was lost. Norway, dependent upon the Hanseatic monopoly of grain, lost the most, and the League became a state within a state. Timbered Hanseatic warehouses by the waterfront in Bergen are reminders of this period.

Queen Margrethe I of Denmark (1352–1412) married King Haakon of Norway and, by the Union of Kalmar (1397), succeeded in uniting all three Scandinavian countries. Norway and Denmark were to remain united until 1814, but Danish rule was much resented in Sweden which finally broke away and re-established her independence under Gustavus Vasa (1523–60). He set about improving Sweden's economic and military strength, peppering the landscape with mighty castles in the process; he also broke with Rome and adopted Lutheranism.

Rising tension erupted in a series of wars between Denmark and Norway on the one hand, and Sweden and Finland on the other. The power of the Hanseatic League was beginning to decline and Denmark gained strength because of her control of the Sound; no ship could enter the Baltic free of her toll. Sweden, on the other hand, held a meagre ice-free outlet to the North Sea, a mere 11 miles of coastline around Gothenburg which, in spite of being defended by the great fortress of Elfsborg, was several times lost to the Danes.

In 1448, the House of Oldenburg had succeeded to the throne of Denmark; now represented (since 1972) by Queen Margrethe II, it is the oldest royal dynasty in Europe. Under one of its early kings, Christian IV (1588–1648), Denmark enjoyed a period of particular prosperity and glory. Despite his robust way of life (he had a great weakness for the fair sex), he was an energetic and competent administrator and much loved by his people. It was he who was responsible for some of Copenhagen's finest buildings, including two royal palaces. He also founded countless new towns in Denmark, Norway and south Sweden, fortified Denmark's frontiers, started trading companies, promoted exploration and improved education and agriculture.

Alas, he was too ambitious and, by bringing Denmark into the Thirty Years' War, he suffered defeat first at the hands of the Germans, and later the Swedes. For Sweden, too, had the benefit of energetic and powerful kings. She achieved her greatest gains under Gustavus II Adolphus (1594–1632) who brought Sweden into the Thirty Years' War on the side of the Protestants and spread Swedish rule to Poland, the Baltic States and parts of Prussia, making the Baltic almost a Swedish lake for a time. By about the middle of the 17th century, Sweden had also finally driven Denmark from the Scandinavian peninsula and had annexed much of western Norway, including a stretch of her western coastline around Trondheim. When Carl (Charles) XII ascended the Swedish throne, he inherited a stable and solvent regime, but much of Sweden's power was lost as a result of the Great Northern War (1697–1718). At first Carl was successful against Peter the Great, but he was defeated in his disastrous march on Moscow. During his many years of absence abroad, Denmark attacked south Sweden once again but unsuccessfully. Later Carl invaded Norway, but was killed by a stray bullet, and Sweden subsequently lost much of her empire.

At the dawn of the 19th century, Napoleon was to turn much of Europe into a battlefield. Gustavus IV, then king of Sweden, bitterly opposed the conqueror, but it served him ill for, following a secret treaty with Napoleon, Czar Alexander I was free to annexe Finland which, in 1809, after more than 600 years of Swedish rule, became a Grand Duchy of Russia; subsequent Czarist oppression eventually resulted in a great Finnish national revival. Meanwhile Denmark and Norway were involved on the side of France; the fierce bombardment of Copenhagen by the British was one repercussion. In the end Sweden's contribution was recognized at the congress of Vienna (1814–15) and, as compensation for loss for Finland, Norway was ceded to Sweden. Denmark, however, continued to control an increasingly unwilling Iceland, as well as Greenland and the Faroes. Ironically, with no heir to succeed Gustavus IV, Jean-Baptiste Bernadotte, one of Napoleon's most talented marshals, was elected Crown Prince of Sweden. The line is currently represented by the seventh ruling Bernadotte, Carl XVI Gustaf who came to the throne in 1973.

The Norwegians profoundly resented Swedish domination, though it was soon to become a fairly loose tie, and they gained complete independence in 1905. Prince Carl of Denmark was elected King Haakon VII of Norway and was succeeded on his death in 1957 by the present king, Olav V.

Scandinavia remained neutral during World War I. Following the Russian Revolution, Finland declared her independence in 1917 and, after some internal struggle, took her place among the responsible small nations of the world. Iceland, formerly a Danish possession, became a sovereign state in 1918 while retaining a personal union with the Danish king; in 1944 she became an independent republic. The Faroes, though still part of the Danish kingdom, became self-governing in 1948. Greenland established Home Rule in 1979.

At the outbreak of World War II, the countries of northern Europe announced their intention to remain neutral, but in November, 1939, the Soviet Union launched the Winter War against Finland. In the peace treaty of March, 1940, Finland had to cede considerable territory to her opponent. In April, 1940, Germany invaded and occupied Denmark and Norway, the latter after considerable resistance. The Faroes and Iceland were occupied by the British in order to forestall German invasion. In 1941, the United States took over the defence of Iceland and still have a base at Keflavik.

In June, 1941, after Germany's invasion of Russia, Finland entered the war in her wake in the hope of regaining lost territory. She was forced to sign a separate treaty with the Soviet Union in September, 1944, losing again much of her eastern territory, her northern outlet to the Barents Sea and was also faced with massive war reparations. Only Sweden had been able to maintain neutrality.

THE ARTS

Despite its small population, Scandinavia has made a brave contribution to the collective creativity of the world; this often reflected the darker and more dramatic moods of its landscapes, the elements and human struggle, though quite frequently with an injection of wry humour. In modern times, few other parts of the world have made more impact on architecture and design.

Literature Runic inscriptions, from the 9th–12th centuries, giving factual details about the personalities and events of the times are the first evidence of writing. It was towards the end of this period that the greatest Norse contribution to world literature was first committed to paper. The Sagas, which for generations had been perpetuated orally, were concerned variously with historical record, romances of chivalry and mighty family epics describing lives and feuds in the 10th and 11th centuries. Most of them come from Iceland and they make robust reading. The outstanding literary figure of those times was **Snorri Sturluson** (1179–1241) whose *Heimskringla* is a history of the kings of Norway up to 1177 and whose Prose Edda covers everything from a comprehensive survey of Norse mythology to advice to young *skálds* (poets).

Apart from a wealth of ballads and religious writings, there followed a considerable gap until the 18th and especially the early 19th century, when a new sense of national identity began to emerge, along with a growing political awareness, in the less independent countries. The 18th-century humorist and philosopher **Ludvig Holberg** (1684–1754), who was born in Norway but spent most of his life in Denmark, is considered the founder of modern Danish and Norwegian literature. The religious–philosophical works of Danish **Søren Kierkegaard** (1813–55) earned him an international reputation, but it was the subtle fairytale world of **Hans Christian Andersen** (1805–75) that first gave Denmark an everlasting place in world literature.

In Norway, **Henrik Wergeland** (1808–45) wrote prolifically and fought passionately for his country's independence, but it was **Henrik Ibsen** (1828–1906) who translated social, religious and moral problems into literary themes and became a model for playwrights the world over. His contemporary, **Bjørnstjerne Bjørnson** (1832–1910), was also profoundly concerned with justice and human rights. Across the border, **August Strindberg** (1849–1912) brought Sweden squarely into the international arena with plays and novels that ranged from bitter misogyny to religious mysticism. Even more popular within Sweden was **Selma Lagerlöf** (1858–1940) who graphically portrayed e in the province of Värmland.

In Finland, a young doctor called **Elias önnrot** quietly collected together the lk tales published as the *Kalevala* 1835, an epic of homeric proportions hich was to help galvanize his country- en into a new awareness of their own ulture. *Kalevala's* influence was far- aching on literature, music and art of the 9th century. First of the great Finnish riters, though he wrote in Swedish, was **ohan Ludvig Runeberg** (1804–77), ut **Aleksis Kivi** (1834–72) was the first ovelist and playwright to write in the innish language and is regarded as the ther of Finnish literature; his works ave an earthy quality that seems to come raight from the forests.

Among other leading Scandinavian riters of the late 19th or 20th century are enmark's **Karen Blixen** (writing as **Isak inesen**), Finland's **Väinö Linna**, Ice- nd's **Halldór Laxness**, Norway's **Knut amsun** and **Sigrid Undset**, and Sweden's är **Lagerkvist**.

Music The two giants of Scandinavian usic are the Norwegian **Edvard Grieg** 1843–1907) and Finland's **Jean Sibelius** 865–1957); the works of both show a rong national flavour. Also important is enmark's **Carl Nielsen** (1865–1931), a omposer of independent style and strong elody.

Folk music and ballads are kept alive hroughout the area, and a number of ajor festivals are devoted to them, as ell as many local events. The tradition is articularly strong in the fjords and valleys f Norway – the distinctive *Harding- ele* (violin with two sets of strings) or which there is no written music, origi- ated there.

Art The art of the area began with primi- ive rock carvings from the Stone Age notably in north Norway) and Bronze Age especially in south Sweden). The Vikings roduced richly carved ships, sledges and rtefacts, their entwined plants and ani- als eventually merging with the motifs of hristianity, for example, in elaborate hurch carvings (notably the Norwegian tave churches, see also Architecture). edieval churches show examples of wall aintings and frescoes. Later came the de- ghtful folk art decorating walls and furni- ure, such as the *rosemaling* (rose painting) hich originated in Telemark, Norway (p. 3) and the charming, god-fearing peasant rt of Dalarna, Sweden (p. 109), with its iblical scenes. Dalarna also produced two mportant painters, **Carl Larsson** (1833– 919) and **Anders Zorn** (1860–1920),

and to the same period belong the more sophisticated works of **Prince Eugen** (1865–1947).

Sometimes described as the father of Danish painting, **Christoffer Wilhelm Eckersberg** (1783–1853) pioneered the naturalism that dominated art in the 19th century. His work was roughly contem- porary with the serene classicism of the sculptor **Bertel Thorvaldsen** (1770– 1844). There were many good, if not internationally known, painters in the 19th century, but when it comes to the international scene, it was Norway that produced one of the first great expres- sionist painters, **Edvard Munch** (1863– 1944, p. 83). In Finland, the *Kalevala* (see Literature) was making a profound impact on art, and notable painters from that period are **Albert Edelfelt** (1854–1905) and **Akseli Gallen Kallela** (1865–1931).

Scandinavian sculptors have proved particularly successful. The works of **Gustav Vigeland** (1869–1943), which occupy an entire park in Oslo (p. 83), are moving and disturbing. Those of **Carl Milles** (1875–1955) are more exuberant and fill his own beautiful terraced gardens in a suburb of Stockholm (p. 113). A controversial painter and sculptor is Denmark's **J.F. Willumsen** (1863– 1958), to whom a museum is devoted in Frederikssund. The works of Finland's **Wäinö Aaltonen** pepper his homeland, while more recently there are fine works by **Aimo Tukiainen** and **Eila Hiltunen**.

The works of both **Jóhannes Kjarval** (1885–1972) and **Ásgrímur Jónsson** (d. 1958), who was much preoccupied with Iceland's exotic natural phenomena, are worth seeking out in Reykjavik, as are the sculptures of **Einar Jónsson** (d. 1954) and Ásmundur Sveinsson.

Architecture Until recent times, Scandi- navian architecture followed in the wake of the rest of Europe, with local variations – the most striking example from early times is the medieval stave church of Norway, with its multiple rooflets adorned with dragon's heads strongly reminiscent of Viking figureheads. For a long time, timber was the main building material and whole towns were destroyed by fire with unfortunate regularity. Rather early, however, the Danes learned how to make bricks which became the princi- pal building material in that country. Gradually throughout the area wooden houses, churches and fortifications were replaced by more enduring stone, and the successive influences of Gothic, Renaissance, Baroque and Rococo filtered northwards.

Around the turn of the century, there was a passionate flourishing of national Romantic styles, especially in Finland which was restlessly establishing its own identity under Czarist rule. Leading names from that period are **Lars Sonck** (1870–1956), **J.S. Siren** (1889–1961) and, most prolific of all, **Eliel Saarinen** (1873–1950) who designed Helsinki Railway Station and town halls all over Finland. It was about the same time that **Ragnar Östberg** was creating Stockholm's imposing City Hall, and a few years later that **Magnus Poulsson** and **Arnstein Arneberg** began work on that of Oslo; both buildings house major contributions from the artists of each country.

The paramount feature of Scandinavia's modern architecture is the successful combination of grace, function and harmony with surrounding nature. There are many outstanding examples created by a considerable list of leading architects in each country, but undoubtedly the most famous name of all remains Finland's **Alvar Aalto** (d. 1976) whose schools, homes and public buildings are dotted all around the world, as well as in many cities, towns and villages in his native land.

PAPERWORK

(See also If you are Motoring, p. 16)
The whole area forms a passport-free zone which means that the citizens of any of these countries do not need passports to visit others within the area and non-Scandinavians need normally show their documents only on entering and leaving the zone. Visas are not required by British or North American visitors.

UK visitors A standard British passport (valid 10 years) is issued after application on the form obtainable at any main post office. This will give the addresses of the Passport Offices in London, Liverpool, Peterborough, Glasgow, Belfast and Newport, Gwent, to which the application should be sent. Two regulation photographs and proof of identity, plus endorsement by a person of standing are required. British Visitor's Passports are also valid for periods not exceeding three months in any nine-month period. The completed BVP application form should be taken by the applicant to a main post office in England, Scotland or Wales (*not* mainland Passport Offices), or, in the case of Northern Ireland, to the Passport Office in Belfast.

US visitors United States citizens whose last US passport was issued within the past 8 years and after their 18th birthday may apply by mail to their nearest Passport Agency

for a new passport. US Domestic Passport Agencies are located in: Boston, Chicago, Detroit, Honolulu, Houston, Los Angeles, Miami, New Orleans, Philadelphia, San Francisco, Seattle, Stamford and Washington. All others must appear personally at the nearest Passport Agency (parents may make applications on behalf of children under the age of 13). Each application must be accompanied by the applicant's latest US passport (or US birth certificate if no previous passport has been held), two identical regulation photographs and the passport fee.

Health There are no special requirements for visitors from the UK or North America either on entering Scandinavia or on return to their own country. Within Scandinavia the medical services are subsidized to various degrees and guidance is given on p. 26. If in doubt that you will be adequately covered, despite the moderate costs likely to be involved in case of need, the small premium required for insuring against risk of illness or injury is a wise investment. American visitors in particular should check that their health insurance policy offer them adequate coverage for illness or accident when abroad.

Insurance of property is also advisable: loss or theft should be reported to the police and a copy of the report obtained to satisfy your insurers.

CUSTOMS

The normal concession for UK visitors to Scandinavia (except Denmark) is 1 litre of spirits, 1 litre of wine, and 200 cigarettes or 250 grammes tobacco. Travellers resident in non-European countries may bring in double the quantity of tobacco. In the case of Denmark, which is a member of the European Economic Community, UK and other EEC residents may bring in 1½ litres of spirits, 5 litres of wine and 300 cigarettes or 400 grammes tobacco. A special facility in Iceland is that you may buy duty-free goods at Keflavik International Airport on entering as well as leaving the country. Note that the minimum age for bringing spirits into Scandinavia is 20 years (Denmark 17 years).

Every country has its list of restricted goods, few of which are likely to affect the law-abiding visitor. If you are on a self-catering holiday, note that for most of the area you may bring in up to 15 kilos of food per person, which should not include fresh, frozen or smoked meat or fish. You are safe with all forms of tinned goods, as well as tea, coffee, dried soups and vegetables, cereals, sugar and biscuits. Some restrictions (dried milk in Norway, potatoes in Sweden) are rather unexpected so, if in doubt, check.

There is a fairly high sales tax throughout Scandinavia, which can be avoided on purchases to be exported (see Shopping, p. 27–8). The chart below indicates what travellers may bring home free of duty.

Duty-free allowances *subject to change*		Goods bought in a duty-free shop	Goods bought in EEC
Tobacco	Cigarettes	200	300
	or		
	Cigars *small*	100	150
	or		
	Cigars *large*	50	75
	or		
	Pipe tobacco	250 gm	400 gm
Alcohol	Spirits *over 38.8° proof*	1 litre	1½ litres
	or		
	Fortified or sparkling wine	2 litres	3 litres
	plus		
	Table wine	2 litres	5 litres
Perfume		50 gm	75 gm
Toilet water		250 cc	375 cc
Other goods		£28	£207

Double if you live outside Europe

US customs permit duty-free $300 retail value of purchases per person, 1 quart of liquor per person over 21, and 100 cigars per person.

CURRENCY

Travellers' checks are the safest. Uniform Eurocheques backed by a guarantee card issued by most UK clearing banks are accepted in banks and establishments displaying the 'EC' symbol throughout the area. Although accepted in many places, indicated by display, international credit cards are not so widely used, especially in Iceland and Norway, as in some other parts of the world. The units of currency and normal banking hours for each country are given below, but much longer hours apply to international airports, main railway stations, harbours and certain exchange bureaus in main cities, while in rural areas the hours may be much more restricted. Money can usually also be exchanged in hotels or at local tourist offices (except Finland) outside banking hours, though the rate given will often be a little lower and, especially in Finnish and Swedish hotels, substantially so. Reasonable amounts of local currency can be taken out of each of the countries, but if large sums are involved you should check current regulations. **Denmark** 1 krone, plural kroner, divided into 100 øre. Banks open 0930–1600 Mon.–Fri. (0930–1800 Thurs. in Copenhagen); closed Sat. **Finland** 1 markka, plural markkaa, divided into 100 penniä. Banks open 0930–1600 Mon.–Fri.; closed Sat. **Iceland** 1 króna, plural krónur, divided into 100 aurar. Banks open 0930–1530/1600 Mon.–Fri., 1000–1200 for foreign exchange only on Sats. in summer. **Norway** 1 krone, plural kroner, divided into 100 øre. Banks open 0815–1530 Mon.–Fri. (0800/0815–1700/1800 on Thurs. in main cities); closed Sat. **Sweden** 1 krona, plural kronor, divided into 100 öre. Banks open 0930–1500 Mon.–Fri. (0930–1700/1800 on Thurs. in main cities); closed Sat.

HOW TO GET THERE

National tourist boards provide a list of tour operators featuring their countries. A selection of specialists is given on p. 29, but the situation is subject to change. Addresses of the following carriers are also given on p. 29.

By Air The only country imposing a separate airport tax is Iceland and this is fairly high. Note that there are many reduced return fare variations, such as Pex, Apex, Super Apex, Eurobudget, and the current situation should be checked. Regular services are far too numerous to be listed, but the following airlines provide direct links. **From the US** Finnair, Icelandair, Northwest Orient, SAS. Note the advantageous stop-over arrangements in Iceland when travelling between the US and Europe. **From the UK** The main operators are British Airways, Finnair, Icelandair and SAS; in addition, smaller airlines such as Air UK, Dan-Air and Maersk operate useful links including a number to and from provincial airports at both ends.

By Sea Denmark Harwich–Esbjerg, year round, or Newcastle–Esbjerg, summer only, 20 hours (DFDS Seaways); Harwich–Hirtshals, year round, 25 hours (Fred Olsen Lines). **Faroes** Aberdeen–Lerwick, Shetland (P & O Ferries)–Tórshavn, summer only (Smyril Line), total 45 hours. **Finland** Harwich–Hamburg, Germany (DFDS Seaways)–(bus)–Travemünde–Helsinki (Finnjet), year round, total approx. 48 hours; UK ports–Helsinki cargo-passenger service, 3 days (United Baltic Corporation). **Iceland** Aberdeen–Lerwick, Shetland (P & O Ferries)–Tórshavn, Faroes–Seydisfjördur (east coast), summer only (Smyril Line), total approx. 60 hours. **Norway** Harwich–Kristiansand, summer only, 24 hours (Fred Olsen Lines); Harwich–Oslo (via Hirtshals, Denmark), year round, 36 hours (Fred Olsen Lines); also connecting services Hirtshals–Kristiansand (Fred Olsen Lines); Newcastle–Bergen/Stavanger, 19/26 hours, summer only (Norway Line). **Sweden** Harwich–Gothenburg, year round, 24 hours, or Newcastle–Gothenburg, summer only, 25 hours (DFDS Seaways).

Note that some of these services can be used in conjunction with onward travel to neighbouring countries by means of the inter-Scandinavian ferries mentioned on p.15. If you are travelling through Germany, you should check other services linking North Germany with several Scandinavian ports. There are also some interesting sea links to Poland from Sweden and Finland, and Estonia from Finland (visas essential).

There are no direct passenger sailings from North America to Scandinavia.

By Road/Sea All the services listed above carry cars. Under certain conditions, usually if accompanied by four full fare-paying passengers, cars travel free on routes to Scandinavia and North Germany. You can, of course, make use of the shorter sea crossings, such as Harwich–Hook of Holland (Sealink), Felixstowe/ Dover–Zeebrugge (Townsend Thoresen), Sheerness–Vlissingen (Olau Line), Ramsgate–Dunkirk (Sally Line). Through fares to Norway and Sweden are quoted on several of these routes.

There are regular coach services from London to Stockholm (Grey Green Coaches, Knightscroft Travel), Gothenburg and Malmö (Grey Green Coaches). The Finnish bus company, Pohjolan Liikenne, operates a year-round service between Gothenburg and Helsinki using the Viking Line Stockholm–Turku route.

By Rail The Eurail Pass (1st and 2nd class) and Eurail Youthpass (for under 26s, 2nd class only) are valid for unlimited rail travel in most European countries (including Scandinavia), but can only be purchased outside Europe. Valid for one month of unlimited rail travel in most European countries (but excluding the issuing country) are the fixed-price Interrail Youth Card for under-26s and Rail Europe Senior Pass for men over 65 and women over 60 (holding a UK Senior Citizen Rail Card). These may be used to obtain big reductions on many cross-Channel services.

The principal routes are as follows; advance bookings and seat reservations are necessary. **Denmark** London (Liverpool St. Station)–Harwich–Esbjerg–Copenhagen, 27 hours; Newcastle–Esbjerg–Copenhagen, 25 hours; London (Liverpool St. Station)–Harwich–Hook of Holland–Copenhagen, 23 hours; London (Victoria Station)–Dover–Ostend–Copenhagen, 22 hours. **Finland** As for Copenhagen or Stockholm, and then by one of several ferries (see p 15), 2–3 days. **Norway** As for Copenhagen and then, via Helsingør–Helsingborg–Gothenburg, 10 hours to Oslo. **Sweden** As for Copenhagen and then, via Helsingør–Helsingborg, 8 hours to Stockholm, or 5 hours to Gothenburg.

Finland, incidentally, has rail connections with the Soviet Union, twice daily from Helsinki.

INTERNAL TRAVEL

An extremely varied transport network exists to link communities across the considerable distances and often difficult terrain of Scandinavia. All the national tourist boards provide full information; see also Tourist Cards, p. 28.

Air In Denmark, Norway and Sweden domestic services are operated by SAS in cooperation with smaller airlines (Danair in Denmark, Braathens-SAFE in Norway, Linjeflyg in Sweden); in Finland

Finnair, and in Iceland by Icelandair ~~with~~ Nordair and East Air. An ever-changing variety of reductions applies to domestic and inter-Scandinavian fares and it is essential to check the latest situation. ~~N~~ote that some of these apply only if ~~tic~~kets are bought outside Scandinavia; ~~ot~~hers only if bought within the area. ~~A~~s a guide, reductions or special flat rates ~~ar~~e likely to apply in the following cir~~c~~umstances: (1) if you travel on off-peak ~~fli~~ghts to some destinations; (2) if you ~~ar~~e a family group with one or more chil~~dr~~en under 26; (3) if you are under 24–26 ~~ye~~ars (depending on country); (4) if you ~~ar~~e not less than 60–67 years (depending ~~on~~ country).

The following specific concessions also ~~ap~~ply: **Denmark** free onward travel from ~~C~~openhagen within Denmark if the ticket ~~we~~re bought before leaving the UK, pro~~vi~~ded there is no break of journey in ~~C~~openhagen. **Finland** unlimited travel for ~~5~~ days using the fixed-price Finnair Holi~~da~~y Ticket. **Iceland** reductions on round-~~Ic~~eland and four-sector trips; also air/bus ~~c~~ombinations. **Norway** discounts include ~~V~~isit Norway Pass on Braathens-SAFE ~~ro~~utes.

~~R~~ail For international rail passes, see p. ~~1~~4. In addition, there is the fixed-price ~~N~~ordturist Railpass valid throughout ~~D~~enmark, Finland, Norway and Sweden ~~fo~~r 21 days of unlimited travel (1st or 2nd ~~cl~~ass), also giving 50 per cent reductions ~~o~~n many inter-Scandinavian shipping ser~~vi~~ces. Groups of from 2 or 3 travelling ~~to~~gether qualify for reductions, but details ~~va~~ry in each country. Children travel half ~~p~~rice or free, but the age range varies ac~~c~~ording to country. There are also dis~~c~~ounts for over-65s in many cases. Other ~~c~~oncessions are as follows, but as these are ~~li~~able to change, you should check the cur~~re~~nt situation as well as any special excur~~si~~on fares which may apply on specific ~~jo~~urneys. **Finland** The fixed-price Finnrail ~~p~~ass gives unlimited travel for 8, 15 or 22 ~~d~~ays and is available to foreigners on show~~in~~g their passports. Tourist tickets com~~bi~~ned with other forms of travel also give ~~re~~ductions, but must be booked ahead. ~~I~~celand No railways! **Norway** Reductions ~~o~~n one-way journeys on several days of the ~~w~~eek allow breaks of journey and are es~~pe~~cially worthwhile on long journeys. ~~S~~weden Swedish State Railways have ~~so~~me remarkable bargains, such as a 25% ~~re~~duction on all 2nd class fares except on ~~F~~ridays and Sundays, and a price ceiling ~~fo~~r long distance journeys of 900km/566mi ~~an~~d over. A 14- or 21-day 'go-as-you-please' ~~ti~~cket on the scenic Inlandsbanan line ~~G~~ällivare–Kristinehamn) affords unre~~st~~ricted travel and many discount facilities.

Bus This is the best method of travel for getting in touch with the countryside; in many areas it is the only one. In all cases there are reductions for children. **Finland** There is an intensive network of regular and express (small additional charge) bus services, supplemented by the mail-carrying yellow postbuses that reach the remotest areas. There are reductions for family groups (minimum 3) and for over-65s who have bought the special 65 Card (photo and passport needed). **Iceland** The fixed-price Omnibus Passport entitles you to unlimited travel by scheduled services for periods of one week to one month. The Full-Circle Passport provides the freedom of a trip round Iceland without time limit. There are also air/bus combinations. **Norway** Bus services are privately run on a regional basis and usually take over where rail or boat services stop. Reduced fares apply to over-67s. **Sweden** Express and regular bus services are supplemented by the mail-carrying yellow postbuses which penetrate the remotest areas. Special excursion tickets give good rates in certain regions. Over-65s get reductions.

Ferries (see also Inland and coastal waters, below) Scandinavia has probably the most intensive and efficient network of drive-on drive-off ferries of any area in the world. Below is a summary of the inter-Scandinavian routes, but check the latest situation. **Denmark–Faroes** Esbjerg–Tórshavn (DFDS Seaways); Hantsholm–Tórshavn (Smyril Line). **Denmark–Norway** Copenhagen–Oslo (DFDS Seaways); Frederikshavn–Oslo (DA-NO Linjen, Stena Line); Frederikshavn–Larvik (Larvik Line); Frederikshavn–Fredrikstad (DA-NO Linjen); Frederikshavn–Moss (Stena Line); Hanstholm–Egersund/Kristiansand (Fred Olsen Lines); Hirtshals–Bergen/Egersund/Kristiansand/Oslo/Stavanger (Fred Olsen Lines). **Denmark–Sweden** Allinge (Bornholm)–Simrishamn (Bornholmstrafikken); Copenhagen–Malmö (hydrofoil, passengers only); Dragør–Limhamn (Scandinavian Ferry Lines); Frederikshavn–Gothenburg (Stena Line); Grenå–Helsingborg/Varberg (Lion Ferry); Helsingør–Helsingborg (Scandinavian Ferry Lines, DSB/SJ); Rønne (Bornholm)–Borgholm (Ölandsborg Rederi); Rønne (Bornholm)–Ystad (Bornholmstrafikken); Tuborg Havn (Copenhagen)–Landskrona (Scarlett Line). **Faroes–Iceland** Tórshavn–Seydisfjördur (Smyril Line). **Faroes–Norway** Tórshavn–Bergen (Smyril Line). **Finland–Sweden** Eckerö (Åland)–Grisslehamn (Eckerö Linjen); Helsinki–Stockholm (Silja Line, Viking Line); Jakobstad (Pietarsaari)–Skellefteå (Jakob Lines); Kokkola–Skellefteå (Jakob Lines); Mariehamn (Åland)–Stockholm

(Birka Line); Naantali–Mariehamn–Kapellskär (Viking Line); Turku–Mariehamn–Stockholm (Silja Line, Viking Line); Vaasa–Sundsvall/Umeå (Vaasaferries).

The following guidelines apply within each country. **Denmark** There are 46 domestic ferries, a number of them operated by Danish State Railways, with various possibilities for combining connecting crossings for through-tickets, or return tickets valid for alternative services. Car fares usually include the driver. Off-season fares are lower and quite a few special offers apply on certain routes at certain times. A free leaflet *Car ferries*, revised annually, is available from the Danish Tourist Board listing all domestic and international services. **Finland** South west Finland is linked with the Åland islands as follows: Turku–Mariehamn (Silja Line, Viking Line); Naantali–Mariehamn (Viking Line). **Sweden** There are regular links with Visby (Gotland) from Nynäshamn, Västervik, Oskarshamn and Grankullavik (Öland).

Inland and coastal waters (see also Ferries, above) **Finland** Many regular services and cruises in summer on Finland's labyrinthine waterways offer possibilities ranging from a few hours by hydrofoil or motorship to one- to seven-day cruises. Meals and refreshments are available on board. The season is normally from late May to late August and main routes are mentioned in the gazetteer. Waterbus trips operate out of Turku to coastal and island communities. Regular services offer opportunities to visit Gdansk (Poland) and Tallinn (Estonia in the Soviet Union) from Helsinki (visas required). **Iceland** A cargo–passenger service operates clockwise and anticlockwise round Iceland, but no advance timetable is published and details must be checked in Reykjavík. **Norway** An 11-day round trip Bergen–Kirkenes–Bergen via the North Cape operates year round with almost daily departures, calling at several ports each day. It can be done in sections or in its entirety, providing an unforgettable cruise. There are also many shorter fjord cruises and an intensive network of regular ferry services in all the fjord districts, linking like clockwork with bus or rail services, through often spectacular scenery. The principal inland waterway routes are on the Telemark Canal and Lake Mjøsa. **Sweden** The famous Göta Canal (p. 99) links Gothenburg and Stockholm in three days by motorship. Other regular summer services include a delightful archipelago route down the east coast from Öregrund, north of Stockholm, to Öland island (regular land links to Stockholm). From Gothenburg and especially Stockholm sight-seeing boats and regular ferries link the cities with extensive archipelagos.

Taxis A roof sign 'Taxi' (*taksi* in Finland) is lit when the vehicle is free. Charges are fairly high and, except in Denmark, there is an additional charge in the evening or at night and, in some cases, at weekends. See also Tipping (p. 28).

Organized excursions During the summer there is a wide variety of organized excursions from all main cities and resorts but at other times of the year organized sightseeing is limited to the capitals and one or two main cities. With advanced planning, combination tickets using various forms of public transport, according to season, offer plenty of year-round possibilities.

IF YOU ARE MOTORING

Driving in Scandinavia is mostly untaxing and traffic is light (at times nonexistent!) except near main cities or resorts at holiday times. Allow plenty of time for covering long distances through often rugged country. Members of their own national motoring organizations may find they can take advantage of certain extra facilities offered by those in Scandinavia (see Useful Addresses, p. 29).

Documents UK visitors taking their own car will need their British driving licence (not a provisional) plus, in Iceland, an International Driving Permit; car registration certificate; an oval national identity sticker (GB or equivalent); and insurance certificate. Though the International Green Card of Insurance is no longer compulsory, it is highly recommended and may save inconvenience in the case of accident. It can be obtained from your insurance company by paying a small extra premium. You should, in any case, check that your insurance cover is adequate for your needs, including damage while in transit.

Rules of the Road

You drive on the right and give way to traffic from the right unless it is clearly marked that you have priority. This also applies to traffic on roundabouts. Trams (and their passengers) always have priority. Pedestrians at crossing places have right of way over traffic, including filter traffic.

Road standards Free maps from the national tourist boards clearly mark major and minor roads. In **Denmark**, all roads are asphalted and well maintained. There are quite a few stretches of motorway and no toll charges; however, remember there are many ferries and costs can quickly mount up. In **Finland**, **Norway** and **Sweden**, main and many secondary roads are excellent. In the far north and remoter areas, surfaces may be oil-gravel or gravel but well maintained. Take special care in the spring thaw (also in Iceland) when some roads are closed for a time and some sections may be pitted with potholes. In Norway especially, many mountain roads are closed in winter, sometimes until late into spring. There are few stretches of motorway except near some main cities and no toll charges, except on the Oslo–Drammen motorway in Norway and a number of minor roads in the Norwegian mountains. Short river-ferry crossings are usually free, but on longer journeys, especially through the fjord systems of Norway, fares, though heavily subsidized, can mount up. In **Iceland**, very few stretches of road are asphalted. Take great care at unbridged rivers which may look more easily forded than they are. In the interior, roads are only passable by 4-wheel drive vehicles and closed until early or mid-July. The Iceland Tourist Board's free *How to travel in the Interior of Iceland* booklet is invaluable.

Road signs These are mostly international and easy to follow. In **Finland**, **Norway** and **Sweden**, unusual hazards are elk or reindeer on the roads (depicted pictorially) and encounters have resulted in nasty accidents especially at dusk. In **Iceland** the hazard is more likely to be cattle, horses and especially sheep.

Lights Headlights for left-hand traffic must be adapted with some opaque material. During the day, dipped head-lights must be used in poor light, mist or fog in **Denmark** and **Norway**; additionally at all times outside built-up areas in **Finland** regardless of conditions, and in all circumstances, year round, in **Iceland** and **Sweden**.

Safety (see also Lights, above). The carrying of a warning triangle, the use of seat belts by drivers and front-seat passengers, and the wearing of crash helmets by motorcyclists are compulsory throughout the area. The use of the horn is only permitted in order to avert danger; headlights should be flashed instead.

Breakdowns The general recommendation in the many sparsely populated areas is to stop the next car for assistance in reaching a garage or telephone. Any breakdown service received must be paid for. For emergency numbers see p. 26. **Denmark** There

are emergency telephones on motorways at frequent intervals. If you cannot drive to a garage, call Falck or Dansk Autohjaelp, both operating a 24-hour service. **Finland** There are emergency telephones on main roads. Autoliitto (Automobile and Touring Club of Finland, ACTF) operates a road patrol service (vehicles carry a yellow roof sign). **Iceland** The Icelandic Motoring Club (FIB) operates patrols at weekends in summer. **Norway** There are many emergency telephones on main roads and in mountain areas, and limited road patrols operated by the Norwegian Motoring Club (NAF) in summer. NAF also runs a 24-hour breakdown service through local garages, though it may be quicker to contact one of the latter direct. **Sweden** Emergency telephones on main roads are limited. A 24-hour service is operated by Larmtjänst (Alarm Services), a central breakdown organization run by insurance companies. There is also a 24-hour emergency garage service in most towns.

Spares and repairs Servicing and minor repairs can be carried out in most places and major repairs in towns. There may, however, be difficulty in getting spares for cars of British make in Norway and Sweden. It can be worth renting a spares kit from your motoring organization or garage, who should also be able to rent out warning triangles and emergency windscreens. A set of spare bulbs should be carried. The following additional items are recommended by the Automobile Association: a pair of windscreen wiper blades, a length of electrical cable, an inner tube of the correct type, a roll of insulating or adhesive tape, a torch, a fire extinguisher, and a tow rope.

Speed limits: Denmark 50kph/31mph in built-up areas, otherwise 80/50 on the open road or 100/62 on motorways; maximum for trailers 70/43. **Finland** 50kph/31mph in built-up areas; otherwise 60/37, 80/50, 110/68 or 120/74 as indicated. If not indicated, the basic limit is 80/50, which is also the maximum for trailers. **Iceland** 50kph/31mph in built-up areas, otherwise 70/43. **Norway** 50kph/31mph in built-up areas, 80/50 on the open road, 90/56 on motorways; maximum for trailers 80/50 with brakes, 60/37 without brakes. **Sweden** 30kph/19mph in school areas, 50/31 in built-up areas; otherwise 70/43, 90/56 or 110/68 as indicated. Maximum for trailers 70/43 with brakes, 40/25 without brakes.

Drinking and driving The law is very strict, the penalties for breaking it severe and there are many spot checks. The legal maximum throughout is 0.5‰ of alcohol in the blood, except in Denmark where it is 0.8‰; less in the case of accident. In short, if you drink don't drive.

Parking Look out for signs incorporating the word *forbudt* or *förbud*, meaning prohibited. Parking is only a problem in a few main cities. Sometimes restrictions apply on even/uneven dates or to house numbers; if in doubt, check for there are many variations. If restrictions are ignored, the car may be towed away or a heavy fine imposed. **Denmark** Limited waiting is always indicated on signs, and parking discs are then required (available from filling stations, banks, tourist offices); otherwise use a parking meter or multistory car park. **Finland** There are meters and a few multistory car parks. **Iceland** There are meters, but parking is rarely a problem. **Norway** Parking is mainly on meters, also a few multistory parks. **Sweden** There are meters and multistory parks; parking is relatively easy but expensive.

Fines Speeding and parking offences are the most common and speed checks are rather frequent. In **Denmark**, on-the-spot fines are imposed and, if not paid, the car may be impounded. In **Finland**, **Norway** and **Sweden** you are given a ticket which must be paid at a post office.

Tyres Remember that your tyres must still meet the legal requirements at the end of your journey and, if in doubt, replace them. If you are travelling in winter, spiked or studded tyres may be used when conditions require it, normally from early or mid October to mid or late April, according to area (rarely required in Denmark). Spiked tyres must be fitted to all wheels. Chains may be necessary if tyre equipment is not adequate for winter conditions.

Vehicle width The normal maximum is 2.5m/8ft 2 in. The exception is in **Norway** where it is 2.3m/7ft 5in for trailers (caravans). If your trailer does not conform to this rule, you should apply for a special permit to Vegdirektoratet (Roads Directorate), PO Box 6390, Etterstad, Oslo 6. This office publishes a leaflet *Caravanning in Norway* available from the Norwegian Tourist Board.

Fuel In **Denmark** (except on motorways) and in the more populated southern regions of **Finland**, **Norway** and **Sweden**, filling stations are plentiful. In the remoter areas and **Iceland**, it is highly advisable to keep your tank topped up. The grades normally available are 92/93, 96 and 98/99 octane, except in Iceland where fuel, imported from the Soviet Union, is never higher than 94 octane. Some garages, especially in Denmark and Sweden, use automats for which you will need bank notes of certain denominations. Lead-free petrol is fairly widely available.

Accidents See also Breakdowns, above, and p. 26 for emergency numbers. If you are involved in an accident, you must stop. Place a warning triangle on the road at an effective distance and seek medical assistance for any injured persons. If required by law, report to the police, leave the vehicle where it is and make sure that all essential particulars are noted. Should it be causing a serious obstruction, mark its position before independent witnesses. If possible, take a photograph of the scene. Check your insurance policy and notify the company within 24 hours in writing. **Denmark** Exchange details with anyone else involved and contact the police. If you are wholly or partly responsible, get in touch with Dansk Forening for International Motorkøretøjsforsikring, Amaliegade 10, 1256 Copenhagen K. **Finland** It is a legal requirement to seek medical help if necessary; if you do not, you are liable to prosecution. Before major repairs, report to Liikennevakuutusyhdistys (Finnish Motor Insurers' Bureau), Bulevardi 28, Helsinki 12. **Iceland** Report to the police in the nearest community; a passing motorist will invariably stop and give you a lift. **Norway** The only firm rule is that, in the case of injury, medical assistance must be obtained and the police called. **Sweden** It is not obligatory (though advisable in your own interests) to call the police, but you are legally required to give your name and address to other persons concerned before leaving the scene of the accident, however slight. Failure to do so makes you liable to prosecution.

Car rental This is widely available, usually at main airports, railway stations and through international or local firms (the latter may be cheaper). It can also be arranged in advance through tour operators specializing in Scandinavia. Car rentals booked with flight reservations on domestic flights are often cheaper, also for rail travellers at some stations.

Car-carrying trains These operate, some seasonally, on the following routes: **Finland** Helsinki–Joensuu/Kajaani/Kolari/Oulu/Rovaniemi; Kouvola-Kolari/Rovaniemi; Kuopio–Rovaniemi; Tampere–Kolari/Rovaniemi; Turku–Rovaniemi. **Sweden** (summer only) Gothenburg–Luleå, Malmö-Umeå, Stockholm-Kiruna.

WHERE TO STAY

There is no official classification of **hotels**, but standards are high. Annually revised lists of hotels and, in most cases, all other forms of accommodation, are distributed free by the national tourist boards. These lists give details of the amenities of each establishment as well as prices, clearly owing whether local taxes, services, *etc*, e included. Central accommodation-ooking offices are maintained, usually in ain railway stations, with long opening ours throughout summer. Local tourist ffices will always assist with advice and, ften, make bookings.

A Bonus Pass scheme of vouchers offer-g 15–40 per cent reductions in many rst-class hotels in Denmark, Finland, orway and Sweden operates from mid ne to end August, and can be purchased rough several UK agents. Other schemes e mentioned under each country below, ut the latest situation should be checked ith each national tourist board. In many ses, there are reductions for children aring parents' room. Substantial savings ually apply to minimum stays of 3 to 5 ys. Two other types of establishment mmon to much of the Nordic area are e Mission Hotels, run by religious organ-ations, usually of good standard though ainly unlicensed; and Summer Hotels, sing school or university accommodation, hich is normally modern, functional, and ften run by the students. Self-catering commodation is extremely well organized roughout most of the area, but expect ur shopping bill to be 15–20% higher an at home.

Note that **youth hostels** in the Nordic untries are open to all age groups, but ou are usually required to be a member of ur national or the international youth ostel association, or to take out temporary embership on the spot. Sleeping bags are ot usually allowed (except in Iceland other an Reykjavik) so you will need a sheet eeping bag (which can sometimes be nted).

Campsites in the Nordic countries are lassified according to a one- to three-star ystem. Usually you are required to hold n international FICC camping card (not Norway), or you may take out a national amping card on the spot. On many sites, ough to a lesser extent in Finland and e remoter parts of Norway, there are ectricity and sometimes water and mains ewage link-ups to trailers (caravans). Many sites also offer accommodation in uts or chalets.

An often misunderstood feature of the Iordic countries is 'all-man's-right' by vhich free use of the countryside is avail-ble to all, especially in Finland, Norway nd Sweden. This right, alas, has been bused by some visitors and, as a result, wild' camping is often discouraged and nay arouse mistrust in some localities. Basically the 'right' entitles you to walk cross or pitch your tent (but not trailer) n uncultivated land, at least 150m/160yd om any habitation, though you should

not stay longer than two days without con-sent of the landowner except in remote areas. You are, of course, expected to cause no damage, leave no rubbish and to observe all the normal courtesies of quiet and orderly behaviour. Camp fires are nor-mally strictly prohibited.

If you are using butane gas, please note that bottles may be refilled or replaced only in a *very* few places at present and you are strongly advised to bring sufficient supplies or to check current availability with the national tourist boards. Alterna-tively, inexpensive, expendable bottles of other liquid gas are available for attach-ment to camping equipment sold in the Nordic and most other European countries.

Denmark You can buy fixed-price Dan or Budget hotel cheques, according to your budget. A characteristic feature of the Danish scene is the *kro* (inn), often a charming, half-timbered building offering traditional decor and food. Many take part in the economical Danish Inn Holiday Scheme: vouchers are valid at any of those participating (leaflet from the Danish Tourist Board). Particularly well organ-ized are the farmhouse holidays, now es-tablished many years, offering full- or half-board accommodation on working farms all over the country. Visitors normally eat with the family and often participate in activities about the farm. It is an ideal holi-day for those with children, travelling by car. Stays are usually for a minimum of one week and can be booked, including travel arrangements, through several UK tour operators (addresses p. 29). There are also plenty of opportunities for self-catering either in small individual cottages or in holiday centres which combine apartments or cottages with restaurant and recreational facilities. Accommodation in private houses is available, usually through local tourist offices. You can get a free list of youth hostels from the Danish Tourist Board; a more detailed guide is on sale locally. Also free from the Danish Tourist Board is a list of the 500 camp sites approved by the Danish Camping Council; a detailed guide can be bought.

Finland A hotel cheque scheme called Finncheque operates in many hotels of various categories throughout the country from 1 June to 31 August; details are given in a leaflet from the Finnish Tourist Board. Several hotel groups, such as Arctia Hotels, Point Hotels, Rantasipi Hotels and Scanhotels, may offer special packages. Inexpensive accommodation is available in a limited number of boarding houses (*matkustajakoti*) bookable through the cen-tral accommodation-booking office in Helsinki railway station or local tourist offices. The latter may also have details of limited private accommodation. Farmhouse holidays, with full- or half-board, are becoming increasingly popular and are described in a separate free leaflet. This also applies to self-catering accommodation in summer cottages and holiday villages, mostly idyllically situated by a lake or seashore amid the forests. You can choose an inexpensive cottage with very basic amenities or a sophisticated log cabin with every modern facility. A free leaflet lists both the 160 youth hostels and 350 campsites. Youth hostels are often in empty schools, and meals are not usually provided, though refreshments are often available and, in some, self-service kitchens.

Iceland There are several top-class hotels in Reykjavik. Outside the capital, many establishments belong to the chain of Edda hotels, mostly adapted into summer hotels from modern boarding schools. Least expensive in towns are guest houses and private rooms. Farmhouse holidays are becoming popular. About 20 youth hostels offer cheap accommodation to those with sleeping bags. The 70 campsites are mostly fairly basic; otherwise, with a few exceptions (marked *Tjaldsvaedi bönnud* – camping forbidden), you may camp almost anywhere on uncultivated or unfenced land, though near farms permission should be sought.

Norway Inter Nor is an association of first-class hotels, and there are several other groups offering advantageous rates through hotel cheque or pass schemes. Hotels are supplemented by various other establishments such as the guest house (*pensjonat*); tourist hostel (*turistheim*) which normally offers fairly simple accommodation, sometimes with communal kitchen facilities; and mountain lodge (*fjellstue*), usually less elaborate than a hotel though increasingly offering similar standards. Private rooms are best outside main towns and may provide cooking facilities. Farmhouse holidays with full board are becoming popular. Self-catering chalets ranging from the extremely simple to the very well equipped are usually ideally situated for open-air holidays. In north Norway and especially the Lofotens, the *rørbu* (fisherman's shelter) has been adapted for those with a taste for the simple life, but you must bring your own linen and perhaps cutlery. There is a free leaflet combining lists of youth hostels and campsites. Of 80 hostels, some are of an exceptionally high standard; main ones offer full restaurant facilities, but not all have self-service kitchens. Of about 1400 campsites, 600 of the best are affiliated to the Norwegian Automobile Club (NAF; address p. 29) who publish a separate, detailed free list.

Sweden A Swedish Hotel Cheque scheme operates in about 180 hotels in two different categories throughout the country from 1 June to 1 September. Some of the participating hotel chains, such as Inter S, Scandic, RESO, SARA and Sweden Hotels, may also offer their own separate packages, as also Countryside Sweden, a consortium of leading country hotels. Other forms of accommodation include the guest house (*pensionat*), mountain hotel (*fjällstation*) and, cheapest of all but excluding breakfast, private room (*rum*). A special scheme, Biltur-Logi 'Hotel Passport', is designed for those on touring holidays and seeking budget bed-and-breakfast rates. Farmhouses usually offer bed and breakfast, though some offer full board, and are booked through local tourist offices. Self-catering accommodation ranges from the simple and isolated cottage to well-equipped chalets in leisure centres with shops and sports facilities. A network of 300 youth hostels (*vandrarhem*) is run by the Swedish Touring Club; standards are high. There is no free list, but an annual guide can be bought giving full details. A free list of campsites is issued by the Swedish National Tourist Office from whom the much more detailed annual *Camping Book*, with nearly 700 sites, can be bought.

FOOD AND DRINK

Scandinavian family meal times are early. Lunch is from 1100/1200–1300/1400 and dinner 1600–1900, though hotel or restaurant evening meals are later – any time from 1800 or 1900. Within these time margins, the Finns and Norwegians eat the earliest, the Danes the latest. Most Scandinavians don't bother much with lunch and usually take sandwiches to their places of work, a fact that is reflected in the vast assortment of sandwiches available in snack bars and restaurants. The Scandinavian sandwich (Danish *smørrebrød*, Finnish *voileipä*, Norwegian *smørbrød*, Swedish *smörgås*) is in a class of its own. It is an open sandwich topped with an enormous choice of fish, meat, cheese, salad and different garnishes, decoratively arranged on a variety of breads. The talent for making food look attractive applies to all meals.

À la carte eating is expensive, but set meals at set prices between fixed hours bring costs down sharply, usually comprising a main dish, salad, soft drink and coffee. In Denmark look out for the Dan Men sign, in Norway for the bear symbol. Take aways are on the increase in all countries. In Finland, the free *Lappi à la Carte* leaflet describes three gourmet routes through Lapland. Service is always included (see Tipping, p. 28).

Breakfast is normally served from 0700/0730 onwards. Most hotels offer the choice of a continental breakfast, but the traditional Scandinavian breakfast is much more substantial. The Danes include a delicious selection of sweet cakes or pastries, though some places now offer the extensive 'cold table' favoured in other parts of Scandinavia. If you travel by sea you will certainly get a good introduction to this gastronomic phenomenon, and it is such a major feature of Scandinavian eating that it requires some explanation.

The 'cold table' (Danish *koldt bord*, Finnish *voileipäpöytä*, Norwegian *koldtbord*, Swedish *smörgåsbord*) is literally a table bearing many different cold items from which you make your selection, returning as often as you like. The dishes reflect the rich harvests yielded by sea, river and lake, the game and fruits of the forests and mountains, as well as the more usual products of farm and market garden. The breakfast version is relatively modest; it will probably include the much-loved salted herring, ham and possibly other cold meats, cheeses, tomatoes, eggs, cereals and different breads. There will be an inexhaustible supply of coffee, milk and various skimmed or sour milks, yoghourt, and tea (which a surprising number of Scandinavians prefer, even though it is invariably the tea-bag variety). It is quite sensible to stoke up at breakfast time and dispense with a big lunch.

The cold table at main meals is a majestic sight, groaning under the weight of dishes. Though there are variations from country to country, and from region to region, you are likely to come across most of the following items at some time or other: lobster, smoked or dill-cured salmon, smoked trout, prawns, shrimps, pickled or cured herring marinated or in a variety of sauces, fried Baltic herring (herring is particularly popular), smoked eel, thinly sliced roast beef, veal, pork, smoked reindeer meat, reindeer tongue, ham, liver pastes, tomatoes, onion rings, egg, pickled cucumber, gherkins, beetroot, and many preserves such as cranberry or red whortleberry. Cheeses include imitations of popular foreign kinds such as Stilton, Gruyère, Camembert, but there are also local varieties – Danish blue, sweet soft goat's cheese and even, if you are bold, the exceedingly strong *gamalost* ('old cheese') of Norway. All these are readily available in food shops and make tasty and inexpensive buys to take home. When it comes to desserts, the emphasis is on creamy soufflés, tiered cakes and a variety of soft fruits and berries, among which the greatest delicacy is the cloud-berry from the northern marshlands.

A gastronomic highlight of the Finnish and Swedish summer is the crayfish, a delicacy harvested from shallow streams and eaten in their thousands during a fixed period in July and August. Restaurants advertise special crayfish evenings and supply diners with decorative bibs as it's quite a messy business for the uninitiated. The crayfish are accompanied by aquavit, beer or white wine, so it is usually a convivial occasion too. In Denmark, Limfjord oysters are highly prized.

Many of the cold table ingredients are translated into delicious hot dishes. Salmon comes in many forms. Fillet of reindeer or young elk or ptarmigan in a cream sauce can be extremely good. Cream sauces are widely used, often incorporating the delicately flavoured mushrooms of which Scandinavia has many varieties. Among less expensive dishes are the ubiquitous spiced meatballs, pea soup with pork (traditionally followed by pancakes), and a whole range of fish such as cod, haddock, coalfish and mackerel. Norwegian *lutefisk* (cod steeped in a lye of potash) is definitely an acquired taste, as is Finland's *kalakukko* (fish and pork baked in a kind of pie). Icelandic specialities include smoked lamb (*hangikjöt*), dried fish (*hardfiskur*) and splendid curds (*skyr*). Potatoes are most often boiled, sometimes served with dill. Fresh vegetables are not so common, but a flourish of lettuce, tomato, beetroot, gherkin may well accompany a hot dish.

Coffee (usually strong, black or with cream) is drunk throughout Scandinavia; cold milk is also popular. Excellent lager-type beer of various strengths is widely available; the famous Danish beers are the best, but there are good ones throughout the area, except in Iceland whose beer is almost non-alcoholic. Local spirits are aquavit (*snaps*) and vodka of various kinds, though imported spirits are very popular (and very expensive). Imported wines, often bottled within each country, are relatively inexpensive. Some interesting liqueurs are distilled from the northern berries, notably from Arctic bramble, cloudberry and cranberry.

Licensing hours: Denmark Alcohol of all kinds is served at any time during opening hours, which are liberal. **Finland** Only beer is served before noon; after that all forms of alcohol are served until closing time. **Iceland** Only very mild beer is available; licensing hours for all forms of alcohol are 1200–1430 and 1900 to closing time, but no spirits at all are served on Wednesdays. **Norway** Beer or wine is available at any time; spirits are only available after 1500 (1300 in resort hotels),

except for Sundays and on certain holidays, when beer or wine only is served.
Sweden No alcohol is served before 1200 (1300 on Sundays) after which it is freely available until closing time.

Alcohol may be bought from many shops in Denmark; its sale in Finland, Iceland, Norway and Sweden, however, is a state monopoly. State monopoly shops are fairly widespread in Sweden and Finland, less so in Norway (there is a dearth in some resorts), and Iceland has very few. Beer is available in some supermarkets and cafeterias in Finland, Norway and Sweden.
Note the strict laws regarding drinking and driving (p. 17–18).

ENJOY YOURSELF

The best source for detailed information is always the national tourist board or local tourist office. The general information brochures published annually by each tourist board, for example, outline the facilities for many special interests and addresses of appropriate organizations can be obtained from them. Leaflets on individual sports are mentioned below; many others are published by local tourist offices. Annual lists of specialist tour operators in the UK are available from national tourist offices – a selection is given on p. 29.
Bathing There is an enormous choice of sea- and lake-bathing and, though water temperatures may not match the Mediterranean, Nordic days can be warm, golden and up to 24 hours long, depending on latitude. Anti-pollution programmes mean that you can sea bathe in the heart of cities such as Helsinki and Stockholm. There are vast stretches of sandy beach along the west coasts of Jutland (beware of tides and currents), Sweden and Finland. But predominant in many areas of Finland, Norway and Sweden are the smooth granite rocks sloping gently down to lake or sea, ideal for walking and sunbathing on and swimming from. Another feature is space. Except for parts of the Danish coast and a handful of popular centres elsewhere in high season, seclusion is there for the asking. Outdoor and year-round indoor pools are common; many in Iceland are fed by natural thermal springs, making winter bathing a particular pleasure. A Danish Tourist Board map marks private and public beaches where nude bathing is practised; the Swedish Tourist Board can provide a list of many naturist clubs. In Finland nude bathing, an intrinsic part of the lake- or sea-side sauna (pp. 23, 53), is never 'mixed' in public saunas.
Canoeing This is a very popular sport in Scandinavia and canoes and/or kayaks can

be rented in many centres. Individual packages including rental of canoe and camping equipment are arranged, for example, in the Jutland lake district of Denmark, and through the Dalsland and many other waterways of Sweden. There are guided trips, with rented equipment through many remoter areas, such as central and northern Finland, on Lake Femund in eastern Norway, and the Dalsland and Värmland districts of Sweden (rafting, too; information from Swedish Touring Club).
Cruising See Inland and coastal waters (p. 16).
Cycling Rental of cycles is widespread and usually arranged through hotels and local tourist offices. Well-organized cycle packages for individuals are marketed by tourist offices, especially in Denmark (*Cycling Holiday in Denmark* pamphlet from Danish Tourist Board) and Sweden (information from Swedish Touring Club; also separate leaflets for Stockholm and various holiday areas); these usually include cycle rental, accommodation with half- or full-board, ferry tickets where necessary and detailed routes. Planned cycle routes or packages are also available in many parts of Finland. If you bring your own cycle, it travels free on some North Sea ferries; there is a charge, however, on Scandinavian trains, not all which can take them.
Field Studies The best-organized guided tours for those interested in bird-watching plants or geology, take place in Iceland which publishes several leaflets on its natural history. Otherwise there is good bird-watching in many coastal and mountain areas of Scandinavia, and many nature reserves can be visited (usually closed in the breeding season). Birding tours are marketed to Denmark, Iceland and Sweden.
Fishing The varied waters and low level of pollution make Scandinavia a paradise for the fisherman. In all cases, local tourist offices should be consulted about permits and local regulations which can be quite complex. Broadly speaking, a local permit is required in all countries, plus a national permit in Finland and Norway for fresh water fishing. Charges are normally very reasonable, though as elsewhere salmon fishing is expensive, if superlative, in some of the rivers of Iceland and northern Scandinavia. Denmark scores best for coarse fishing in Jutland. Fishing from the seashore is usually free, but a permit may be required. Stockholm is probably unique among capitals for the fishing from its bridges in the city centre, even resulting in salmon. Tackle can be rented from sports shops and some hotels; tackle imported into Iceland and Norway must be disinfected

following free leaflets are useful: *...ing (Finland), Salmon and Trout Fish-...in Iceland, Angling in Norway, Fishing ...e Stockholm Region, Angling in Sweden.*

...f This is especially popular in Denmark ...courses) and Sweden (187 courses). ...re are quite a few clubs in Finland, ...ral near main towns in Norway and ...owing number in Iceland. Visitors are ...e very welcome.

...ging The boom is evident in most ...dinavian centres, many of which offer ...llent jogging tracks.

...ing There are horse-riding schools ...ughout the area and sometimes ...ngements can be made through ...ls. In Norway, riding tours through ...mountains are run by the Norwegian ...intain Touring Association. In ...den, the best areas are Värmland ...Dalarna. The sport is particularly ...ular in Iceland whose small sturdy ...ses, directly descended from their ...ing Age ancestors, can be booked ...day- or longer tours. They have their ...special gait adapted to the rough ...ain.

...ing The fragmented coasts and scat-...d archipelagoes of Scandinavia offer ...erb sailing, as do some of the innumer-...e lakes. There are leaflets summarizing ...regulations and amenities for those ...aging their own vessels into Danish and ...dish coastal waters. No special restric-...s apply, though you must, of course, ...ply with the customs regulations of each ...ntry. Bear in mind the strict rabies laws ...26). Rental of yacht or motor cruiser is ...ely available in Denmark and Sweden ..., to a lesser extent, in Finland and ...rway. There are also some sailing schools ...ich arrange courses. Flotilla sailing is ...w well established in Finland.

...na This remarkable cleansing and ...ial institution originated in Finland ...ere it remains an intrinsic part of the ...y of life (p. 53). It has spread widely ...ecially throughout her Scandinavian ...ghbours, though the authentic Finnish ...cle is rarely matched elsewhere. The ...erience is at its best in a lake- or sea-...re sauna when it can be combined with ...mming and relaxation overlooking ...nquil scenes. Contrary to popular be-..., public saunas are never 'mixed'; there ...certain hours for men or women, though ...st saunas can also be booked for private ...ups.

...nnis Available at many clubs, ...els campsites, *etc*, in Denmark, Nor-...y and Sweden and, to a lesser degree, ...Finland.

...lking and Climbing Few areas of the ...rld offer wilder and more varied walk-...country and the amenities with which

to enjoy it to the full. Be warned, however, that there are many areas of Finland, Iceland, Norway and Sweden where you should *never* strike out alone unless you are fit, experienced and well equipped. Always ask for local advice and follow it, and always tell the hotel, hostel, campsite, *etc*, in which direction you are heading and when you intend to be back. Opportunities are endless and the following are only a few guidelines. **Denmark** Special events are the organised walks or marches in which many thousands participate each year. Most are for one day, but some are longer; the best known is a 2-day event from Viborg, in Jutland, in June. **Finland** An excellent booklet *Hiking Routes* outlines in English 24 marked trails throughout Finland rang-ing from 7–85km/4–53mi in length. Guided hiking tours are arranged. **Iceland** Many guided treks and camping tours through parts of Iceland's extremely rugged interior are arranged, with camping equipment provided or available for rent. **Norway** There are over 20 mountain areas with cairned or marked trails and tourist chalets (with or without warden) spaced a day's walk apart. Unique are the self-service huts with blankets, food, wood, paraffin, and set charges (posted up inside) which you pay according to what you use. These provide truly remarkable possibilities for walking in remote mountain areas free of heavy packs. The huts are run by the very active Norwegian Mountain Touring Association, who can also supply all in-formation on maps, guided tours, climbing and glacier courses, dog-sleigh touring in winter, *etc*. **Sweden** There is a number of marked long-distance trails (leaflet avail-able) ranging from the King's Route in the far north (430km/266mi) passing Sweden's highest mountain Kebnekaise, to Sörmlandsleden, south of Stockholm (500km/310mi, divided into 41 stages). One-day walks or full week hiking pack-ages with guide and equipment are organ-ized; details from the Swedish Touring Club.

Water sports Rental of equipment and instruction in water skiing and wind-surfing are widely available in Denmark and Sweden, and opportunities are in-creasing in Finland and Norway. (See also Bathing, Canoeing, Sailing.) Courses in skin diving are confined to Sweden's west coast.

Winter Sports Skiing as a sport was born in Scandinavia: in the Telemark district of Norway. And for several months of the year, Finland, Norway and Sweden be-come to a large extent nations on skis. Their national tourist boards produce ex-cellent leaflets outlining amenities for visitors. Generally speaking, the gentle forested undulations and bare-topped fells of Finland and Sweden, or the grandiose highland plateaus of Norway are best suited to cross-country skiing and there are many marked trails. Cross-country equipment is much lighter than that used for downhill skiing and it can be rented or bought locally, usually inexpensively. In contrast, ski jumping is also very popular. Of recent years, ski lifts and tows have proliferated on the hills of all three countries, but Norway is by far the best developed in its facilities for downhill and slalom, and several resorts are featured in winter packages from the UK. Ski instruction and rental of equipment are available in all three countries. Nearly all centres provide illumination of some trails or slopes in the evening to counteract the short daylight hours of midwinter. Après-ski entertainment tends to be more limited than in the Alpine countries, but there is always dancing in hotels or restaurants. Other winter activities include reindeer safaris, sleigh rides, fishing through holes in the ice, skidoo (motorized sledge) trips, and car racing on ice.

ENTERTAINMENT

Events of special note are mentioned throughout the gazetteer, and each national tourist board publishes a free calendar of events every year. One of the attractions of Scandinavia is the contrast between the modern amenities of even the smallest settlements and the often rugged nature, even isolation, of their settings. Until recent decades, communities had to make their own entertainment, and the many folk traditions that resulted survive to this day in pleasing contrast with the more sophisticated night life and cultural events of the cities. The seasons, too, whose rhythms play such an important part in much of Scandinavian life, are reflected in annual celebrations.

One example is May Day Eve, the Walpurgis Night of German legend called *Valbergsmässoafton* in Sweden and *Vapunaatto* in Finnish. This is as much as anything a welcome to the return of spring and a night, especially, for student pranks. Students and ex-students of all ages wear their graduation caps and splash about in fountains; balloons and other festive items are on sale; hotels and restaurants hold special dances and many people never see their beds this night. The festivities are most assiduously upheld in Finland and Sweden, the latter featuring huge bonfires in many places. Norway, on the other hand, goes to town on 17 May (Constitution Day). For the Danes 1 May means the

official opening of Tivoli and a sure sig that summer is on its way.

Huge bonfires in Denmark, most Finland, Norway and northern Swede signify Midsummer Eve, Scandinavia other great ritual homage to the seasons this time in honour of the year's longe day which, in the far north, is indeed 2 hours long. In Sweden and some weste parts of Finland, the bonfire is replaced a decorated maypole and this really c tradition, complete with folk dancin music and feasting, is the most attra tive of all (an especially lively time in t Swedish province of Dalarna). Again, fe people see their beds this night. Mi winter, too, has its celebrants, though or in Sweden where the Feast of St Lucia 13 December features processions of t Queen of Light throughout the country usually an attractive young lady wearing crown of candles.

Because summer is relatively brief and be enjoyed to the full, there is an empha on open-air entertainment. The adventu park or Summerland (Sommerland), wi wide-ranging family appeal, is popular some areas. Usually the fairly high adm sion fee covers use of the many amenit and attractions. Nearly every town has summer theatre with performances national or foreign plays in the light Nor evenings. The pleasure gardens in seve cities of Denmark (notably Copenhagen Tivoli) and Sweden (notably Gothenbur Liseberg) are splendid places for fam entertainment, ranging from full-scale fu fairs and beautiful floral displays to to class international shows with both popu and classical appeal. Open-air concerts c high standard in city parks or the cou yards of castles and other historic bui ings are many, sometimes even free. Str theatre and musicians proliferate in cit such as Copenhagen, Århus, Stockhol An intriguing part of Sweden's town are open-air chess and other games wh attract small crowds of onlookers on a summer evening. Open-air markets cr the narrow streets of idyllic little towns summer, but occur in winter, too, in m cities where they have their own spe atmosphere as furred and booted st holders stamp their feet in hard-pac snow, often against a backdrop of froz harbour, with the winter sun a hazy ora ball low on the horizon.

Summer displays of folk dancing numerous and there are many folk grou often of professional standard, who ma tain the traditions in each country. Tho attractive regional costumes are no lon worn on an everyday basis, many are to seen on festive occasions. The province Dalarna in Sweden is particularly noted ts strong folkloric tradition, often reflecting the influence of the church, or the *mélange* of the pagan and Christian that is evident in much of rural Scandinavia. The colourful church boat processions of Dalarna are one example, another is the performance of allegorical plays, such as *The Road to Heaven* at Leksand. The mystery pageant *Petrus de Dacia* at Visby on the island of Gotland is a splendid spectacle. In Norway, too, there are many local events such as the peasant-style weddings in Voss and the children's weddings in the Hardangerfjord area, while the Fana folklore evenings arranged regularly throughout summer just outside Bergen are very popular.

In the far north, colourful Same (Lapp) festivals provide opportunities for scattered communities of these distinctive people to get together. Many of these occasions are church festivals, often held on Lady Day or at Easter when the snow is still thick on the ground and the full regalia of the Same costume, with its deep blues bordered with several bands of rich multicoloured braid, makes a splendid blaze of colour. Several weddings will probably take place at these times, as well as sporting events such as lasso-throwing competitions and reindeer races on some frozen lake. Important centres include Karasjok and Kautokeino in Norway, Inari and Enontekiö in Finland. There are also the big winter markets or fairs of the far north, usually in February or March, such as those of Jokkmokk and Arjeplog in Sweden. Denmark's traditional events tend to have a historical flavour. A major event is the Viking Festival in Frederikssund from mid June into early July. Tilting at the Ring festivities, with horse parades and competitions on horseback, are special features of south Jutland towns, especially Sønderborg.

There are several cultural festivals of a more conventional nature and of international standard, combining all kinds of music and drama. Leading events include the Bergen Festival, Helsinki Festival and Århus Festival. There are also many other important events. Jazz, for example, is the theme of an annual festival in Molde, Norway, the Pori Festival in Finland, and the Copenhagen Jazz Festival, while the Roskilde Festival (Denmark) is the biggest of its kind in northern Europe to focus on beat, jazz and folk music. A splendid medieval castle provides the setting for the Savonlinna Opera Festival in Finland, while mainly 18th-century operas unfold throughout summer in the exquisite Rococo theatre of Drottningholm, Stockholm. In Denmark, the children of Odense re-create the famous fairy tales

for the Hans Christian Andersen Festival, and during the Copenhagen Festival, open air entertainment fills the streets, squares and open air stages. In Finland, two special themes are offered in the Kaustinen Folk Music Festival and the Lahti International Organ Festival. Folk songs are also the theme of the Skagen Ballad Festival in Jutland.

Pop and rock concerts and jazz clubs have a great following among the Scandinavian young, and there are plenty of conventional cabaret and discos in the big cities, with Copenhagen in the lead and Stockholm in second place. The popular places get crowded and you may find a burly doorman checking up that latecomers appear desirable and/or properly dressed. This may seem a curious precaution in view of the tolerance shown towards the drinking habits of the 'properly dressed' who have already gained entrance. The tendency of some Scandinavians towards over-indulgence in alcohol is a fact of life, though it is rarely intrusive in the better establishments. In tourist resorts and small towns, there is dancing on most nights in one hotel or more, quite often to a live band. This is a dubious blessing if you want a quiet meal.

Other occasions when you are likely to see the Scandinavians letting down their hair are at major spectator sports events. There is fierce if friendly rivalry between them when it comes to sport, notably football and athletics in summer, and ice hockey, ski jumping and cross-country skiing in winter. Impressive spectacles of a gentler nature are the big sailing competitions (notably the round-Funen and round-Sealand regattas) of Denmark. Every Scandinavian capital now has its Marathon.

WHAT YOU NEED TO KNOW

Chemist Dispensing chemist's (pharmacies) are called *Apotek* in Denmark, Iceland (also *Lyfjaverslun*), Norway and Sweden. In Finland look for *Apteekki*. For normal hours see Opening Times (below), but all main towns will have at least one shop offering a 24-hour service. Your hotel, campsite or the local tourist office can give the address.

Churches Religious services in English are held in all the Scandinavian capitals, at least in summer, except for Iceland (at the Keflavik base only). Details of these and other services for all denominations are given in free local *What's On* publications or are available from local tourist offices; in Norway, services in English are also held in many tourist resorts.

Cigarettes and Tobacco Foreign brands are readily available throughout the area, but are invariably expensive. Note that in Iceland, duty-free tobacco goods may be purchased on arrival at Keflavik Airport

Electricity With very few exceptions the current is 220 volts AC, 50 cycles, but you are likely to need an adaptor for the round 2-pin continental sockets.

Emergencies Emergency telephone numbers for police, fire and ambulance are as follows: **Denmark** 000 nationwide; **Finland** 000 in Helsinki only; **Norway** 000 in Oslo only; **Sweden** 90 000 nationwide. Otherwise check in local directories or with your hotel, *etc*.

Health There is some kind of reciprocal arrangement with Britain throughout the area, but North American visitors especially are advised to take out insurance cover, subject to the comments below, and, if you are on prescribed drugs, make sure you have sufficient supplies with you. Details of concessions for British visitors are given in Leaflet SA30 available from your local Department of Health and Social Security office or the DHSS Overseas Branch, Newcastle upon Tyne, NE98 1YX. In general these are as follows: **Denmark** In emergencies, hospital treatment for all foreigners is free; in other cases UK nationals also get free treatment, but North American visitors should expect to pay. UK nationals should show their passport to the doctor or chemist and, if payment is required, a refund can be obtained from the nearest municipal or health insurance office (address from tourist office). **Finland** Facilities for all foreigners are the same as for Finns, *ie* free use of health centres, a nominal daily charge for hospital inpatients, and a moderate charge for prescribed drugs. **Iceland** UK visitors are entitled to free emergency treatment, and should take their medical card; otherwise, all visitors pay the same as Icelanders. **Norway and Sweden** UK visitors are entitled to free treatment in hospitals (small nominal fee in Sweden) and part refund of doctor's fees as outpatients. Receipts should be taken with your UK passport to the local Social Insurance Office (*Trygdekasse* in Norway, *Försäkringskassan* in Sweden). Charges for prescribed drugs are moderate.

Note that, because of the risk of **rabies**, regulations throughout Scandinavia are extremely strict regarding the import of domestic pets which are subject to long quarantine (except those entering Denmark from the UK).

The UK totally prohibits the importation of animals (including domestic pets) except under licence and involving quarantine in approved premises for up to six months. Penalties for smuggling are severe.

Any animal being imported into the U must have a valid certificate of vaccinatio against rabies.

For further details apply to the Ministr of Agriculture (Animal Health Division Hook Rise South, Tolworth, Surbitor Surrey KT6 7NF.

Information Local tourist offices i Scandinavia are usually exceptionally helf ful and they offer a generous service whic includes booking accommodation, arrang ing excursions and local package tou of general or special interest, changin money if the banks are closed, and gene ally directing your footsteps to the rig source of information or help in almost an circumstance. Many of these offices pub lish annually revised leaflets, often i English, covering a wide range of local in formation. Tourist offices are usuall identified by a small letter 'i', generally i white on a green background; otherwi look out for the following signs: **Denma** *Turistbureau*; **Finland** *Matkailutoimist* **Norway** *Turist informasjon*; **Swede** *Turistbyrå*.

Licensing Hours (see Food and Drink p 21–2)

Lost Property The local tourist office w direct you to the police, railway, city tran port office, *etc*, as relevant.

Mosquitoes These can be a great nuisanc especially in the lake districts or in the fa north, though much less so on the coas Some summers are more afflicted tha others, but the worst period is usual from midsummer to mid August. Repe lents are not infallible, but they do hel seek advice from your chemist or doctor you suffer from allergies.

Museums and Monuments See al Tourist Cards, p. 28. Throughout tH areas there are considerable variations opening times within the range of 100 1100–1500/1700 (or even later), so it is e sential to check locally. Opening hours m be substantially shorter in winter and som museums close for that season. In summ most close one day a week, often Mo: Few museums are free (except in Iceland but entrance fees compare favourably wi those of the UK. Many, even in sm: towns and rural areas, display excelle explanatory texts in English, especial in Denmark and Norway, and in ma: cases guides in English can be boug though they can be quite expensive.

The concept of the open-air museur re-creating communities of the past, com from Scandinavia and many are well wor visiting. When it comes to monuments other man-made traces from the pa Scandinavia scores high in Iron Age fo and burial mounds, mummified bodie ship graves, prehistoric rock carving

king remains, medieval churches, Ren-
sance castles and modern architecture.
rther guidance is given throughout the
zetteer.

wspapers and Radio Foreign news-
pers and books are readily available
bookshops and kiosks in all main cities
d many resort hotels. They are rather
pensive. Some major papers have
nmaries of news in English. English-
guage radio broadcasts (news and
rist information) are transmitted in
ny parts of the area, especially in
mmer.

f-season Throughout most of the area,
e high season coincides with the school
lidays (mid-June to mid-August) and
tside this period prices – and crowds –
e substantially less.

ening Times There are considerable
al variations, but the following are
idelines for main cities.
ops: **Denmark** Mon.–Thurs. 0900–
30, Fri. 0900–1900/2000, Sat. 0900–
00/1400. **Finland** Tues.–Thurs. 0830/
00–1700/1800, Mon. and Fri. 0830/
00–2000, Sat. 0830/0900–1300/1400.
nger hours in subway shopping centre
Helsinki Railway Station. **Iceland**
on.–Fri. 0900–1800, Sat. 0900–1200
me shops close Sat. in summer). **Norway**
on.–Fri. 0900–1600/1700, Sat. 0900–
00/1400. A number of shops in Oslo are
w open 1000–2300. **Sweden** Mon.–Fri.
00/0930–1700/1800, Sat. 0900–1300/
00. Some department stores open to
00/2200 once or twice weekly.

otography the only restrictions are
arly marked: in some museums, near
ilitary installations or anywhere within
me distance of the Soviet border. Some
me (Lapp) people in the far north prefer
t to be photographed; it is courteous to
k them.

lice Throughout the area, the police
iform is dark blue or black, with light
ue shirt and dark overcoat in winter.
vedish road patrols often wear green
eralls. Winter headgear in Finland,
orway and Sweden is a fur hat. Police are
ually friendly and helpful.

stal Services (see also Telephones,
low) Post boxes, usually attached to a
all, are red in Denmark, Iceland and
orway, and yellow in Finland and
weden. Postage stamps are readily avail-
le from hotels, kiosks, tobacconists and
me bookshops as well as post offices.
rmal post office opening hours are given
low, but these will be longer at main
fices in the cities. **Denmark** Mon.–Fri.
00/1000–1700/1730, Sat. 0900–1200;
nland Mon.–Fri. 0900–1700, Sat. closed
xcept main post office); **Iceland** Mon.–
i. 0800/0900–1700, Sat. 0900–1200;

Norway Mon.–Fri. 0800–1700/1730
(summer 1630), Sat. 0900–1200; **Sweden**
Mon.–Fri. 0800/0900–1800, Sat. 1000–
1300 (some branches closed Sats. in July).
Public Holidays The following are public
holidays throughout the area: 1 Jan., Good
Friday, Easter Monday, 1 May (except
Denmark), Ascension Day, Whit Monday,
25 and 26 Dec. Additional ones are:
Denmark Maundy Thurs. (day before
Good Friday), Day of Prayer (fourth Fri.
after Good Friday), 5 June (Constitution
Day), 24 Dec., 31 Dec.; **Finland** Epiphany
(Sat. nearest 6 Jan.), Midsummer Day (Sat.
nearest 24 June), All Saints Day (Sat. at
end Oct. or early Nov.), 6 Dec. (Independence Day), 24 Dec.; **Iceland** Maundy
Thurs. (day before Good Friday), 22 April
(first day of summer), August Bank Holiday (first Mon. in Aug.); **Norway** Maundy
Thurs. (day before Good Friday), 17 May
(Constitution Day); **Sweden** 6 Jan.
(Epiphany), Midsummer Day (Sat. nearest
24 June), All Saints Day (Sat. at end Oct.
or early Nov.). On these days banks, offices and most shops are closed.
Shopping (see also Opening Times,
above) Look out for the annual summer
sales. Scandinavia is famous for design and
quality. Items in glass, ceramics, wood,
stainless steel and also textiles are of a high
standard. In addition, **Denmark** is particularly noted for amber and handmade pipes;
Finland for fashion goods in marvellous
colours; **Iceland** for beautiful knitwear
in natural wool colours, and interesting
lavaware; **Norway** for pewter, silver,
enamelware, distinctive knitwear; **Sweden**
for cut glass and household gadgets.

Traditional crafts and designs drawn
from folk cultures are kept very much alive
and many regional handicrafts organizations ensure high quality. There is also
attractive jewellery, often incorporating
semi-precious stones, extracted, cut and
polished in remoter areas of the far north.
Many museums sell well-made replicas of
ancient artistry. Beautiful furs are also
good, if more expensive, buys. At the
other end of the scale is an enormous
variety of candles which all Scandinavians
put to good decorative use. Some tasty
food and drink items are mentioned in the
section Food and Drink.

A high sales tax (*moms* in Denmark,
Norway and Sweden) is imposed and can
be avoided (except in Iceland) by making
your purchases at shops indicating they
participate in the tax free shopping service;
you will then be entitled to a refund of the
tax on departure. Ask for the special Tax
Free Shopping leaflet for each country as
the details vary and, in some cases, apply
only to purchases above a substantial
minimum value.

Telephones Public telephone boxes are well distributed in town streets. Except for Denmark, you will not find them in post offices but in special Telegraph offices (marked *Tele* or, in Finland *Lennätin*). The procedure is to lift the receiver, insert the money and dial; if you are not connected, the money is returned, except in Denmark where it is therefore advisable to start with the lowest coins. Charges for calls from hotels can be quite expensive. Except in a few remote areas, there is long-distance direct automatic dialling throughout, and also to Britain and North America, though this is not always possible from public boxes. When checking a number in the telephone directory, remember that names beginning with Scandinavian letters such as Å, Ä, Ö, Ø come at the end of the alphabet. In Iceland, entries are under Christian names.

Time Differential Iceland is on Greenwich Mean Time; Denmark, Norway and Sweden are 1 hour ahead; Finland 2 hours ahead. As all, except Iceland, apply 'summer time', the time differential remains the same for most of the year: *ie* Finland is 2 hours ahead of British time, 7 hours behind US Eastern Time; Denmark, Norway and Sweden are 1 hour ahead of British time, 6 hours behind US Eastern time; Iceland is 1 hour behind British time in summer, on the same time in winter, and 4 hours behind US Eastern Time in summer, 5 hours in winter.

Tipping A service charge is included in hotel and restaurant bills throughout the area and extra tipping is not as prevalent as in many other parts of the world. (In Iceland there is no tipping at all.)

Good service in a restaurant is usually acknowledged by sums ranging from a few low denomination coins to, say, 10 per cent depending on the standard of restaurant. It is also usual practice to leave your coat in the cloakroom for which there is a fixed charge, or to tip the doorman a similar sum. Taxi drivers and hairdressers do not expect tips, except in Sweden where 10–15 per cent is considered normal. Railway porters, if you can find them, operate on fixed charges.

Toilets Standards in hotels, restaurants, department stores are generally very high, but those of other public toilets do vary and are not always up to Scandinavia's usual high standard. In some places, especially in rural areas, you may need to ask for the key. The sexes are often indicated by the small figure of a man or woman. Otherwise the words to look out for are: Denmark *herrer*, *damer*; Finland 'H' or *miehille*, 'D' or *naisille*; Iceland *karlar*, *konur*; Norway *herrer*, *damer*; Sweden *herrar*, *damer*.

Tourist Cards The Copenhagen, Helsin Oslo or Stockholm Card (also available some other cities, so it is worth checki locally) can be a good buy. It provi free travel on city transport, entrance museums and many discount facilities f periods of from 1–3 days. Other discou cards offer unlimited travel within cert areas, so it is always worth enquiring local tourist offices what's on offer.

Youth discounts and facilities are me tioned where appropriate, but the Inte national Student Identity Card of Federation of International Youth Tra Organizations (FIYTO) card will op many doors to their holders. The Natio Tourist Offices can give addresses of th respective student organizations.

USEFUL ADDRESSE:

(tel. nos in brackets)

Scandinavian Tourist Offices: U Danish Tourist Board, Sceptre Hou 169/173 Regent St., London W1R 8PY 734 2637); Finnish Tourist Board, Haymarket, London SW1 4RF (01 8 4048); Iceland Tourist Information Bure 73 Grosvenor St., London W1X 9DD 493 4619); Norwegian Tourist Board, Pall Mall, London SW1Y 5NE (01 8 6255); Swedish National Tourist Office Cork St., London W1X 1HA (01 437 58 **USA** All countries: 655 Third Aven New York, NY 10017 (212 949 233 **Canada** Danish Tourist Board, PO F 115, Station 'N', Toronto, Ontario M 3S4 (416 823 9620).

British Consulates: Denmark Kastels 36–40, 2100 Copenhagen Ø (01 26460 also in Åbenrå, Ålborg, Århus, Esbje Fredericia, Odense; **Finland** Uudenma katu 16–20, 00120 Helsinki 12 (90 1257 also Oulu, Pori, Tampere, Turku, Vaas **Iceland** Laugavegur 49, Reykjavik (158 4), also Akureyri; **Norway** Thor Heftyesgate 8, Oslo 2 (02 563890/7), a Ålesund, Bergen, Haugesund, Kristians (N), Narvik, Stavanger, Tromsø, Tro heim; **Sweden** Skarpögatan 6–8, 11 Stockholm (08 670140), also Gothenbu Malmö.

US Embassies: Denmark Dag Hamm skjölds Allé 24, 2100 Copenhagen Ø 423144); **Finland** I. Puistotie 14A, 00 Helsinki 14 (90 171931); **Iceland** Lauga gur 21, Reykjavik (29100); **Nor** Drammensveien 18, Oslo (02 4485; **Sweden** Strandvagen 101, 11527 Stockh (08 630520).

Canadian Embassies: Denmark Kris Bernikowsgade 1, 1105 Copenhagen K 122299). **Finland** Pohjoisesplanadi 2 00100 Helsinki 10 (90 171141); **Nor**

scars gate 20, Oslo (02 466955); **Sweden**
egelbacken 4, 10323 Stockholm (08
37920).

ir Services   Air UK, Norwich
irport, Norfolk NR6 6ER (01 551 4988);
ritish Airways, PO Box 10, Heathrow
irport, Hounslow, Middx. TW6 2JA (01
47 4000); Dan-Air, Newman House,
ictoria St., Horley, Surrey RH6 7QG (01
40 1011); Finnair, 14 Clifford St., London
1X 1RD (01 408 1222); Icelandair, 73
rosvenor St., London W1X 9DD (01 499
71); Maersk Air, Liverpool Street Station,
ondon EC2M 7QH (01 623 3813);
orthwest Orient, 49 Albemarle St.,
ondon W1X 3FE (01 629 5353); Scandi-
vian Airlines, 52/53 Conduit St., London
1 0AY (01 734 4020).

oach services   Grey green Coaches, 53
amford Hill, London N16 5TD (01 800
00); Knightscroft Travel, Lyckas House,
Knightscroft, New Ash Green, Kent
A3 8JS (0474 872160).

hipping services   DFDS Seaways,
andinavia House, Parkeston Quay,
arwich, Essex CO12 4QG (0255 552000);
orway Line, Tyne Commission Quay,
bert Edward Dock, North Shields NE29
A (0632 585555); Olau Line, Sheerness,
ent ME12 1SN (0795 666666); Fred
lsen Lines, 11 Conduit St., London
1R 0LS (01 409 2019); P & O Ferries,
Box 5, P & O Terminal, Jamieson's
uay, Aberdeen AB9 8DL (0224 572615);
lly Line, 54 Harbour Parade, Ramsgate,
ent CT11 8LN (0843 595522); Sealink,
Box 29, London SW1V 1JX (01 834
22); Smyril Line, see P & O Ferries
ove; Townsend Thoresen, 127 Regent
, London W1R 8LB (01 734 4431);
ited Baltic Corporation, 21 Bury St.,
ndon EC3A 5AU (01 283 1266).

otoring Organizations   Automobile
sociation, Fanum House, Basingstoke,
ants. RG21 2EA (0256 20123); Royal
tomobile Club, RAC House, Lansdowne
., Croydon CR0 2JA (01 686 2525);
renede Danske Motorejere (FDM),
egdamsvej 124, 2100 Copenhagen Ø (01
2112); Autoliitto (Automobile and Tour-
g Club of Finland), Kansakoulukatu
, 00100 Helsinki 10 (90 6940022);
orges   Automobil-Forbund   (NAF),
orgate 2, Oslo (02 429400); Kongelig
rsk Automobilklub (KNA), Parkveien
, Oslo 2 (02 562690); Motormännens
ksförbund (M), Sturegatan 32, 10240
ockholm (08 7823800); Svenska Turist-
eningen (STF), Vasagatan 48, 10120
ockholm (08 227200).

me Specialist UK Tour Operators
ecial activities have been specified where
plicable. Angler's World Holidays, 25
arket Place, Bolsover, Chesterfield,
rbyshire (0246 826350), fishing; Branta
Travel, 11 Uxbridge St., London W8 7TQ
(01 229 7231), bird watching; Cox &
King's, 46 Marshall St., London W1V 2PA
(01 439 3380), botany, riding; Danish/
Finnish/Swedish Chalets, 28 Hillcrest Rd.,
Orpington, Kent BR6 9AW (0689 24958);
DFDS Seaways/Longship Holidays, see
Shipping Services above; Each Cycling,
Tempo House, 15 Falcon Rd., London
SW11 (01 223 6966), cycling; Fairways &
Swinford, Sea Containers House, 20
Upper Ground, London SE1 9PF (01 261
1744), botany; Finlandia, 130 Jermyn St.,
London SW1Y 4UJ (01 839 4741); Norway
Line, see Shipping Services above; Nor-
wegian State Railways, 21–24 Cockspur
St., London SW1Y 5DA (01 930 6666);
Fred Olsen, see Shipping Services above;
Dick Phillips, Whitehall House, Nenthead,
Alston, Cumbria CA9 3PS (0498 81440),
walking in Iceland; Ramblers Holidays,
Longcroft House, Fretherne Rd., Welwyn
Garden City, Herts. AL8 6PQ (0707
331133), walking; E. Raymond & Co.,
25 Prudential Buildings, 36 Dale St.,
Liverpool L2 5SW (051 236 2960); Regent
Holidays, 66 Regent St., Shanklin, Isle of
Wight PO37 7AE (098386 4212); Scantours,
8 Spring Gardens, Trafalgar Square,
London SW1A 2BG (01 839 2927); Sonic-
world House, High St., Henfield, West
Sussex BN5 9HP (0273 494081); Sporting
Travel Service, 9 Teasdale Close, Royston,
Herts. SG8 5TD (0763 42867), canoeing;
TTS Tours, St. Nicholas Chambers,
Amen Corner, Newcastle upon Tyne NE1
7PE (0632 329225); Twickenham Travel,
33 Notting Hill Gate, London W11 3JQ
(01 221 7278).

LANGUAGE

With the exception of Finnish, the Scandinavian languages belong to one of three
divisions of the Germanic branch of Indo-
European languages. Despite the quite
marked differences in their languages,
Danes, Norwegians and Swedes can un-
derstand each other with relative ease. In
Norway, the situation is slightly compli-
cated by the fact that, until 1905, when
it seceded from Sweden, the official language was Danish and the current majority
language, called *riksmål* Norwegian (or
'book Norwegian'), is substantially influenced by Danish. About 100 years ago
there began a strong movement to revive
the older Norwegian dialects, now called
landsmål (or 'new Norwegian') and both
are taught in schools and used in government service. *Riksmål* Norwegian still
predominates, however, except in the rural
areas of western Norway.

In the case of Iceland, much greater
isolation has resulted in a language that is

virtually unchanged from the Norse of medieval times, and Icelanders can read their ancient sagas without any problems; you might compare this to a modern English-speaking student being able to read Chaucer with ease. They have also retained the old system of patronymics. Thus Jón Sigurdsson is Jón, the son of Sigurd; his son Sveinn becomes Sveinn Jónsson and his daughter Helga, Helga Jónsdóttir. And so on. Women do not change their names when they marry. so, if you want to trace anyone through the telephone directory, you look for them under their Christian name. There is a strong movement to protect the Icelandic language from the introduction of foreign words.

Swedish is also the second official language of Finland where it is the mother tongue of a minority of about 6 per cent. The Finnish language itself belongs to the Finno-Ugrian group (together, for example, with Estonian and Hungarian) and, with its 14 grammatical cases, appears very difficult, though it is extremely logical and, like the Scandinavian languages, phonetic. Until the national revival movement of the 19th century, Finnish was largely the language of the less privileged. It was the publication of such epic works as *Kalevala* (p. 11) that helped Finns to a new awareness of their cultural heritage.

The alphabet includes a few extra letters: ä (Finnish and Swedish), å (Danish and Swedish), ö (Finnish, Icelandic and Swedish), ø (Danish and Norwegian). Note that these come at the end of the alphabet, an important point to remember when referring to an index or directory. Icelandic also retains two consonants from ancient Norse: ∂ (similar to *d*) and þ (*th* as in thin). Since the pronunciation of certain combinations of letters (such as *sk* before some vowels or *g* at the end of words) varies from one country to another, it is a good idea to learn the basics if only to pronounce place names correctly when seeking directions.

English is very widely taught and spoken throughout Scandinavia, though rather less generally in Finland, especially among the older generation. On the whole, there are few areas of the non-English speaking world where you are less likely to meet language problems.

DENMARK

Denmark's area of approximately 43,000sq km/16,600sq mi is roughly twice the size of Wales and carries a population of about five million. Apart from Jutland, it consists of nearly 500 islands of which 100 are inhabited, giving a total coastlin 7300km/4500mi. Though it lacks the scenic drama of its northern neighbo its countryside is fair and fertile, and relaxed Danes have an easy-going frien ness that is not quite so manifest in t fellow Scandinavians.

Denmark's two highest points (b 170m/557ft) are in east Jutland. By far most predominant features of its la scapes are the undulating, well-husban farmlands punctuated by woods and huddle of pretty villages or farm c plexes, often of considerable age. Ther something timeless and relaxing ab these tidy landscapes, though the win change is in evidence as reduced d herds lead to increasing arable produc and rosy pigs disappear into the w sheds of factory farming. It remains, h ever, an ideal and well-organized cou for the farmhouse holiday with its special family appeal; ideal, too, for mo ists and cyclists for whom there are cellent facilities. Note that the dista given in the gazetteer apply to road tances and time should be allowed for f crossings where appropriate.

There is much to see: rich collecti dating back to prehistory, numerous tra from Viking times, many castles and m asteries reflecting the prosperity of Middle Ages when the great forests w cleared. Christianity was introduced by monk Ansgar (826–865) and the vill church became a major feature of r Denmark along with the half-timbe farms and inns. It was the monks taught the people to burn clay, account for the predominance of brick as a build material throughout the country. L came the castles, manors and parks refl ing and adapting the Renaissance st especially from Holland.

Denmark's other great natural featur the complexity of its coastlines, provid splendid sheltered waters for boati bathing, fishing and other water spo Among the stirring sights of the Dan summer is the fluttering of a my colourful sails during the round-Fu and (especially) round-Sealand rega which attract not only the experts large-scale family participation. A ter trial equivalent are the marches or org ized walks (p. 23) in which many hundr take part.

Culturally there is plenty doing fr jazz and medieval jousting to street thea and the Royal Danish Ballet. Denma pleasure gardens – Copenhagen's Tivol simply the largest and most sophisticate typify the Danish talent for catering for tastes and all ages in the same place at same time.

JUTLAND

...nd is the only part of Denmark at-
...ed to the continent of Europe, a fact
...has caused it many problems through-
...its history. Its southern approach
...ss the narrow neck of flat lands shared
... Germany's Schleswig Holstein has
...ys been vulnerable and the border fre-
...tly disputed. Dutch and German
...itectural influences are very apparent
...e little towns of south Jutland.

...s early as the 9th century, a defensive
...em of earthworks called Danevirke
...w in Germany) was begun by King
...fred to protect his lands from Charle-
...ne. The most recent contest over this
...der was the Danish–Prussian War
...h resulted in much of south Jutland
...g ceded to Prussia in 1864 (part of it
...re-united with Denmark in 1920).
...se territorial losses included Jutland's
...t fertile land. Much of the rest of the
...nsula consisted of unproductive bog
...heath. So serious was this for the
...ntry's economy that the Heath Insti-
...was created to do battle with the
...rland. The reclamation was arduous
...which eventually earned the cultivators
...emorial park near Viborg, but it was
... effective: about 900,000 hectares or
...illion acres (90 per cent) of the moor-
...l was reclaimed, and it is now the turn
...he moorland to be protected by the
...e Institute!

...curious phenomenon of the Jutland
...is its preservative properties; hence
...astonishing number of 'bog people' –
...ses in such remarkable condition that
...r 2000 years they retain, in some cases,
...owth of beard, a profusion of hair and
...n the discernible remains of their last
...l. Notable examples are in Silkeborg
...Århus. Iron Age (*eg* Århus) and Vik-
...finds (*eg* Lindholm Høje, Jelling)
...numerous. Even more numerous are
... stone churches and beautiful half-
...bered buildings from medieval times
...vards, collected into notable open-air
...seums at Hjerl Hede and Århus, but
... to be seen in towns and villages all
...r the peninsula.

...he much-fragmented west coast is an-
...r attraction, with its big lagoonlike
...ds, and the great waterway complex of
...fjord that links the North Sea with the
...tegat. Some of the beaches are unin-
...upted for miles, often firm enough to
...driven on, and backed by rolling sand
...es. Most of Denmark's amber is
...hed up on these beaches, especially
...r autumn storms. The bird life is
...ed, with several nature reserves (*eg*
...perne). Many rivers, flowing in all

directions from the heathery hills, offer
good fishing, and one of them, the Gudenå,
winding northwards to Randers through
the central lake district, provides an idyllic, though sometimes overcrowded,
canoeing route.

Ålborg   F6

(pop. 155,000) Denmark's fourth largest
town faces industrial **Nørresundby** to
which it is linked by bridges and a tunnel
across Limfjord. The centre of the town
has great charm with narrow lanes and
houses from the 15th–19th centuries, notably Aalborghus (1539; once the building
of the royal exchequer), Jorgen Olufsen's
House (1616) and Jens Bang's impressive,
if ostentatious, 5-story Stone House (1624)
next to the Old Town Hall (1762). The
tourist office, opposite the last-named,
makes a good starting point for exploring
on foot and has excellent leaflets to direct
your footsteps. Nearby, the cathedral
(Budolfidomkirke) has been rebuilt and
expanded over 800 years; much of it, including the spire, is Baroque. Helligånds-
sklostret (1431), a monastery sheltering a
home for the elderly, is beautifully preserved. The ultramodern North Jutland
Museum of Art (Aalto and Baruël) has
very fine Danish and foreign collections,
and the Historical Museum includes some
excellent glass and silver. There is also a
large, well-arranged zoo and Tivoliland
pleasure gardens with varied entertainment. This is, indeed, a lively cosmopoli-
tan town with a wide choice of restaurants,
wine bars, discos and night clubs.

In the east part of town is 12th-century
Nørre Tranders Church (stone carvings,
frescoes). To the north overlooking the
industrial landscapes of Nørresundby is
Lindholm Høje, a remarkable Iron Age
and Viking cemetery in which 682 graves
are scattered about a hillside, many of
their stone settings in distinctive boat

shapes. Here, too, is a field bearing the furrows and plough marks of 1000 years ago. The Shagerrak coast, a short drive north west of Ålborg, is a huge expanse of beach fringed with extensive sand dunes; the beach is so firm that you can drive along it for miles, *eg* from **Blokhus** to **Løkken**. A little north east of Blokhus is **Fårup Sommerland** (see p. 24) *Esbjerg 228km/141mi.*

Århus   I7

(pop. 250,000) Founded in Viking times, this is Denmark's second largest city. After a period of stagnation following the Reformation, it rose to become a major trading centre and industrial city with a busy harbour. There are ferry connections with Kalundborg on Sealand. The oldest church is the Church of our Lady (from 1100) under whose choir an 11th-century crypt church was discovered in recent years. The upper part of the interior is Gothic with late medieval frescoes. The cathedral, in the late Gothic style of the 15th century, has the longest nave and biggest organ in Denmark, medieval choir stalls, a fine altarpiece (1479), and many wall paintings.

Occupying part of the Botanical Garden is an outstanding open-air museum, Den gamle By (Old town), a collection of 60 half-timbered town houses and shops from different parts of Denmark dating from 1600–1860. The modern Town Hall has a façade in Greenland marble.

On the north side of town, Århus University is set in rolling parkland. On the south side is the Tivoli-Friheden amusement park and, beyond it, the beautiful Memorial Park, with a monument to World War I, set in beech woods and opening out on to the bay. Nearby, the park of the Queen's summer residence, Marselisborg, with beautiful rose gardens, is open to the public when she is not in residence. Also south of town, in the manor house of Moesgård is an exceptionally fine Museum of Prehistory with collections from the Iron Age (mummified body of Grauballe Man, about 1600 years old) and Viking Age runic stones. A 'prehistoric track' leads from here past sundry original and reconstructed prehistoric structures (dolmens, barrows, houses). *Esbjerg 152km/94mi.*

Ebeltoft   I8

(pop. 3000) The old core of the town is a truly picture-postcard place of cobbled streets lined with half-timbered houses, very well preserved and many from the 16th–18th centuries, including some excellent inns and eating places. A town crier does his rounds every summer evening. This is the main town of the Mols region, characterized by the wooded and heath-

covered Mols hills which offer good wal ing. There are frequent connections wi Sjaellands Odde on Sealand. *Esbje 209km/129mi.*

Esbjerg   L

(pop. 80,000) For many visitors bu Esbjerg provides their first glimpse Denmark, yet not much more than 1 years ago there was little here but a han ful of farms. Esbjerg grew with the dev opment of the harbour from 1868, the rival of the railway, shipping links with t UK and the fishing fleets which tod make it Denmark's largest fishing po The lively goings-on in the Fish Aucti Hall (from 0700) are among Esbjerg's a tractions. It also has a particularly we equipped Fishery and Maritime Museu In 20 minutes by ferry you can reach t holiday island of **Fanø** (pop. 3000; 55 km/21sq mi) with its huge and popu expanses of beach on which it is possible drive for many miles. In its heyday of t 18th–19th centuries, Fanø had a sizea fleet of sailing ships many of whose sk pers lived in the delightful community **Sønderho** in the south of the island. A of the old houses are protected and church is notable for its ship mode **Nordby**, where the ferry lands, is the b gest centre (Fanø Museum). The island innumerable holiday homes. *Copenha 278km/172mi.*

Frederikshavn   I

(pop. 35,000) This is a major port, fish and industrial centre, with regular sea c nections to Norway, Sweden, and Danish island of **Laesø** which is an spoilt haven of meadows, moor and sa dunes, with several pretty churches a seaweed-thatched farms. Frederiksha has some 17th-century houses and 18th-century manor house, Bangsbo, i museum with excellent collections fr the Stone Age to World War II. Acr Jutland's narrow tip, **Hirtshals** has dev oped into a busy small port with regu connections with Harwich and seve Norwegian ports. Its modern North Museum features vast salt water aquariu and seals. *Esbjerg 290km/180mi.*

Grenå   I

(pop. 15,600) This manufacturing town the coast of the peninsula of Djurslan mainly known for its modern harb from which there are car-ferry links w Hundested in Sealand, the islet of Anh and with Sweden. The Djursland count side is charming, dotted with pretty villa and manor houses. The adventure park **Djurs Sommerland** (see p. 24) is a miles west at Nimtofte. **Anholt** cov 22sq km/8½ sq mi with 160 inhabitants

is a haven for escapists seeking peace. There are mini desertlike stretches of drifting sand, stony plains and dunes, and you can cycle or walk all round the island along the beach. *Esbjerg 214km/132mi.*

Haderslev M5
(pop. 30,000) The town sprawls between the head of Haderslev fjord and a lake. It is an ancient market town, with 16th-century houses featuring Dutch-style bay windows, and dominated by its red-brick medieval cathedral. The archaeological collection in the regional museum is particularly fine and includes a copy of the Skrydstrup Girl's dress from about 1300 BC. Old half-timbered farms and other buildings may be seen in the open-air section of the museum. *Esbjerg 80km/50mi.*

Horsens K6
(pop. 45,000) This town on Horsens fjord was a prosperous trading centre in the 18th century, from which time a number of merchants' houses of substance survive. It had developed earlier round its medieval abbey whose church has rich interiors (15th-century carvings). Today there is some industry. *Esbjerg 110km/68mi.*

Kolding L5
(pop. 55,000) Today an industrial town, Kolding began as a medieval fortress, then abbey and trading centre. For centuries, Koldinghus (13th century, but reconstructed after fire), was a royal residence; now it houses a museum and fine library. The Geographical Gardens are notable; plants from all over the world include Northern Europe's biggest bamboo grove and 10,000 roses. *Esbjerg 72km/44mi.*

Mariager H6
(pop. 2000) This is a charming little market town on a fjord of the same name; it developed round 15th-century St Bridget Abbey. There is a number of old churches in the surroundings (**Dalbyneder, Udbyneder** and **Visborg**), but of particular interest is the Viking Age encampment of **Fyrkat** (10km/6mi W) near the small industrial town of **Hobro** (Viking Museum). *Esbjerg 202km/125mi.*

Nykøbing G4
(pop. 9000) The town is the principal community on the island of Mors in Limfjord (bridge and ferry connections). Its heyday was in the 15th-17th centuries, the great period of the herring fishery. Today it is a main centre of the oyster industry for which Limfjord is well known. The 14th-century abbey round which the town

developed is now a historical museu
Esbjerg 164km/102mi.

Rebild National Park
In 1912, Danish-Americans purchased natural amphitheatre in the heathery h of north Jutland and presented it to Danish nation. The Lincoln Log Ca was built to house an Emigrant Museu The celebrations held here each 4 are the biggest anywhere in or out of United States. The surrounding region Rold Forest and the Rebild Hills is v beautiful and includes Denmark's larg woodland area. It is a fine area for walki *Esbjerg 210km/130mi.*

Ribe
(pop. 8250) This is one of the oldest a prettiest towns in Scandinavia, and been an episcopal seat since 948. Its five-aisled cathedral was founded in 12th century on the highest point, thou today the surrounding houses, built o the centuries on successive layers of rubb stand a little above it. There are over protected houses from the 16th-18th ce turies and enormous care is taken to ens that repairs and restorations maintain original styles. The local tourist associat plays a vital part in what is an unusua enlightened programme of urban cons vation, by which private owners may tain interest-free loans provided th restored building is properly maintained

A stroll through the narrow streets w their red-brick, half-timbered or colo washed houses is very rewarding. Bui ings of special note include the Cathed School (Denmark's oldest), the Town H (1528), St Catharine's Church and the lightful convent buildings (1228; n a charitable foundation), and Quede Gaard (museum in a merchant's fo winged house). Every summer evening nightwatchman does his colourful roun In summer you can take a riverboat t from Skibbroen, the old harbour, throu unspoilt marshlands to the sea. the south west, the island of Rø (old church, regional museum) is reach by a 10km/6mi causeway; it is a pla of heath, marsh, extensive sand du and great beaches. *Esbjerg 30km/18mi.*

Ringkøbing
(pop. 6500) This charming little we coast town was an important fishing a cattle-trading centre in the 16th-17 centuries, and its narrow streets a lovely old houses echo those times. T brick church is late medieval, and t museum includes a Greenland depa

rhus

ibe

Lacemaking, Tønder

ment. A few miles north is Summerland West (see p. 24). To the south are the great expanses of the lagoonlike Ringkøbing fjord, separated from the North Sea by the 40km/25mi-long isthmus of Holmslands Klit with its sand dunes, beaches and lively fishing port of **Hvide Sande**. In the south of the fjord is the chunky peninsula of **Tipperne** on which there is one of Scandinavia's top bird sanctuaries (open limited hours without a permit on Sundays). *Esbjerg 80km/50mi.*

Samsø   K8
(pop. 4900) This shoe-shaped island lies about halfway between central Jutland and Funen and is linked to both by ferry. Its 114sq km/44sq mi are quite unspoilt – beaches, rolling dunes and meadowland, and interesting bird life. In the north, **Nordby** is a pretty village of half-timbered farms. In the south is **Brattingsborg**, a 19th-century manor house with English garden. Roughly central, **Tranebjerg** (pop. 660) is the island's biggest community with a museum farm (Samsø Museumsgård) and 14th-century church.

Silkeborg   I5
(pop. 46,500) In the heart of the central

Jutland lake district, Silkeborg is a plea ant small lakeside town. Its Provinci Museum is a gem and contains two Scandinavia's greatest curiosities: Tollu Man and Elling Woman, discovered in remarkable state of preservation in nea bogs. Both died over 2000 years ago hanging, possibly as offerings to a go Tollund Man is the better preserved, h lined face in gentle repose with a day so's growth of stubble. Elling Woman h little face but a fine crop of plaited hai From Silkeborg there are lake tours k paddle steamer and other boats to the fo of **Himmelbjerget**, Denmark's secor highest hill (147m/482ft). The town al lies about halfway along a popular cano ing route, an idyllic, if at times crowde 160km/100mi stretch of river and lal waters from **Tørring** to **Randers**, whic can be joined at Silkeborg. *Esbjerg 139kr 86mi.*

Skagen   C
(pop. 13,000) This is a delightful tow near the tip of Jutland. About 75 per ce of its economy is based on fishing, and th comings and goings of its fishing fleet its fish auctions and the bustle in th harbour are among its great attraction

Rows of little red-painted storehouses from the turn of the century line the quaysides and add to the visual appeal. The way of life of the old days is well preserved in the open-air museum of Skagens Fortidsminder. Skagen became well known throughout northern Europe because of the artists who flocked here in the late 19th and early 20th centuries, attracted by the pure light, the prettiness of the place and the windswept heaths and sand dunes. Many of their works may be seen in the Skagen Museum or in the Brøndum Hotel. Artists include Michael and Anna Ancher, P.S. Kroyer and the Norwegian Christian Krogh. The Anchers' house is also a museum. Painting holidays are arranged by the tourist office each summer.

Grenen, the windswept northernmost point of Jutland, is only 5km/3mi away, with yet another art museum (modern). Here, where the waters of the Skagerrak and Kattegat meet and crash against the long beaches, are several generations of lighthouse. One, near town, is a reconstruction of a 16th-century bascule, or seesaw, light. West of town, the tower of a buried church rises out of the sand. **Råbjerg Mile**, a few miles south west, is an extraordinary expanse of high sand dunes. You can reach it, but only on foot, from nearby **Kandestederne**.
Esbjerg 337 km/209mi.

Skive H4
(pop. 27,000) This small industrial town is on Skive fjord, one of the southern ramifications of the complex Limfjord system. Skive Museum's archaeological collections include Denmark's biggest amber find and an interesting Greenland collection. But the town's main attraction is as a launching point for several places of interest in the Limfjord countryside. **Hjerl Hede** (20km/12mi SW) is an exceptionally fine and still expanding open-air museum set in extensive protected forest and moorland by Lake Flyndersø. It consists of about 40 buildings from different parts of the country, among them Denmark's oldest farm, a church, school, workshops, etc. There is also a Stone Age settlement in which the daily life of 5000 years ago is re-created every July. **Spøttrup Castle** (19km/11mi NW of Skive) is a splendidly restored medieval castle rising out of encircling double moats. *Esbjerg 143km/88mi.*

Thisted F3
(pop. 13,000) In a splendid situation on the shores of Limfjord, this small industrial town has a Renaissance church. The surroundings have yielded many prehis-

toric sites, notably **Ydby Skjold**, a collection of 32 Bronze Age burial mounds near Ydby to the south west. The nearby heath-fringed Skagerrak coast has glorious beaches and from Hanstholm, a few miles north, there are sea links to the Faroes and Norway.
Esbjerg 182km/113mi.

Tønder N4
(pop. 7400) This pretty town, in the centre of a cattle-breeding area and later famous for its lace, has changed hands many times in its history. It has fine houses from the 17th and 18th centuries and a good regional museum illustrating traditional crafts of the area (lace, silver, etc). The church (1592) has a rich interior.
Esbjerg 77km/48mi.

Vejle K5
(pop. 49,000) The town, which developed round the head of Vejle fjord, is mainly interesting for its surroundings of wooded slopes characteristic of east Jutland. There are summer boat trips on the fjord and a veteran railway runs through the pretty Grejs valley. At **Jelling** (11km/7mi W) are the 10th-century royal burial mounds and runic stones associated with King Gorm the Old and his Queen Thyra. One of the runic stones in the churchyard bears perhaps Scandinavia's oldest representation of Christ, surrounded by Viking Age animal decoration. It is dedicated to Gorm by his son Harald Bluetooth 'who conquered Denmark and Norway and made his people Christian'. The church has Denmark's oldest, but restored, frescoes (12th century).

At **Billund** (28km/17mi W of Vejle) is the very different attraction of Legoland, a miniature world created out of 30 million of the famous interlocking plastic components, from Dutch canal landscapes to temples of the Far East. Another popular exhibit is Titania's Palace, originally built by Sir Nevile Wilkinson for his daughter (completed 1922) and quite astonishing in its detail and workmanship. An excellent Doll Museum, a traffic school, Wild West town and pony riding are among other features which make this one of Scandinavia's top family attractions. *Esbjerg 83km/51mi.*

Viborg H5
(pop. 28,000) For about 600 years, until the early 17th century, this ancient town was Jutland's capital. It lies in the central lake district amid rolling farmland. The granite cathedral was built about 100 years ago on the site of a series of earlier churches; its 19th-century starkness was alleviated early this century by the frescoes

of Joakim Skovgaard and his team, who created a kind of pictorial Bible with over 50 scenes. Søndre Sogns Church has been largely restored to its original medieval condition, retaining later valuable additions such as the 18th-century pews embellished with more than 200 paintings. Many of the old red-brick houses of the town centre from the 16th century onwards are being restored; the general effect is charming and well worth some footwork.

At **Kongenshus**, is a memorial park and a museum to the heath cultivators who transformed their unproductive landscapes; here you can see how much of Jutland looked only 100 years ago. This can be combined with a visit to the huge lime pits near **Mønsted** (35km/21mi of galleries) and **Daugbjerg** (probably in use since Viking times), west of Viborg. Viborg is also at the northern end of the old Military Road (*Haervej*), a historic track and now a walking and cycling route which follows the Jutland watershed south to the German border. There is an organized 2-day walk along it in late June. *Esbjerg 155km/96mi.*

FUNEN LANGELAND AERØ

With justification Funen is referred to as 'the garden of Denmark'. Its neatness has a prosperous look drawn from the rich soils and their high yields. Stone walls or hedges add orderliness to the scene, while woods contribute their deeper green flourish. Odense is the main city, made famous by its renowned son Hans Christian Andersen. South Funen and the islands of Aerø and Langeland have the particular charm of areas lying off main through routes.

Aerøskøbing   O7
(pop. 1300) This is the principal community on the island of Aerø, reached by ferry from Svendborg or Fåborg on Funen, and from Monmark, south Jutland. For 500 years the island formed part of Schleswig whose influence is marked in the architectural styles. The island is a delightful rural backwater and Aerøskøbing itself is near-perfect, with nothing to jar the harmony of its tiny streets and half-timbered houses from the 15th–19th

centuries. One of them, the Bailiff's House, contains the Aerø Museum and Old Pharmacy. The post office (1749) is Denmark's oldest. There is also a substantial bottle ship collection.

Egeskov   M7
In the heart of the Funen countryside, this is one of Denmark's worthiest castles and, indeed, one of Europe's best preserved island forts. It was built (1524–54) on a foundation of oak pillars wedged into the bottom of a small lake, so that it rises literally out of the water (access by bridge). With its pink stonework it is a most pleasing sight and its surrounding park is famous for Renaissance, Baroque and modern landscaping, a maze of 200-year-old hedges and a magnificent fuchsia garden. Part of the estate is an ancient barn now containing the Egeskov Veteran Museum of aircraft, cars and other vehicles. *Esbjerg 162km/101mi.*

Fåborg   N7
(pop. 6500) This picturesque old town has ferry connections with Als, south Jutland, the island of Aerø and some smaller islands and Gelting in north Germany. It has many old houses, and a well-preserved west gate, one of few town gates surviving in Denmark. Den gamle Gård museum has interesting local collections, and Fåborg Museum is devoted to the works of Funen painters. The bell tower is from 1475. *Esbjerg 160km/100mi.*

Nyborg   M8
(pop. 14,300) In medieval times, this was the heavily fortified administrative hub of Denmark, seat of parliament and scene of the signing of the country's oldest constitution in 1282. Its 12th-century castle, restored earlier this century, can be visited. From its commanding position on the coast, this splendid pile guarded the Great Belt between Funen and Sealand, though much of its grandeur was lost when King Frederick IV had bricks quarried from its massive walls to build his palace in Odense. Nyborg Museum is in an attractive 17th-century merchant's half-timbered house. From the nearby harbour of Knud shoved there are regular ferry crossings over the Great Belt to Halsskovhavn on Sealand. *Esbjerg 167km/104mi.*

Odense   L7
(pop. 170,000) Odense is Denmark's third biggest city, linked by a 7km/4mi canal to the sea. Today a busy commercial and industrial centre, with a shipyard and brewery, its origins are ancient and its historical and cultural associations many

...geskov Castle

...t has been an episcopal residence since ...020 and St Knud's Cathedral, built in ...e mid 13th century, is a magnificent ...othic building with many interesting ...etails, including a superb carved altar-...iece with 300 figures by the Odense ...aster Claus Berg. Knud (Canute) the ...oly, of tide-commanding fame, was ...illed here and is buried in the fine crypt ...vhich also houses other royal tombs. Also ...f note is St Hans Church, begun in the ...3th century.

Most famous of Odense's progeny was ...Ians Christian Andersen (1805–75), son ...f a shoemaker. His fairy tales enchanted ...he world and have been translated into ...ver 100 languages. The house tradition-...lly believed to be his birthplace has been ...estored and turned into a fascinating ...nemorial, illustrating his life through ...etters, manuscripts, documents, pictures ...nd other memorabilia. It includes the ...runk of this lonely but much-travelled ...nan, and the rope which he always carried ...vith him as a means of escape in case of ...ire. Despite his nervousness and hypo-...hondria, he undertook many hazardous ...ourneys and met a galaxy of literary and ...ristocratic people as evidenced by his ...liaries and correspondence, among which ...re letters from Charles Dickens. Ander-...en fluctuated between delight and des-

pair, yet he saw wonder in the workaday world and made others see it too. The humble house in which he lived until the age of 14 when he left for Copenhagen is also a museum. He loved children, but never married, though he had a deep love and friendship for Jenny Lind, the 'Swedish nightingale'. The Hans Christian Andersen Festival (mid July to mid August) is a delightful re-enactment of his fairy tales by the children of Odense.

Could he return, Andersen would recognize many of the buildings in Odense today. They include beautiful half-timbered houses, well represented in the museum of Møntrestraede, a collection of several 16th- and 17th-century buildings which illustrate the life of those times, including the history of the guild system. In the south part of town, Funen Village is a major open-air museum of old houses showing the peasant culture of the 18th and 19th centuries. Other museums of note are the Fyns Stifts Museum (archaeological finds from the Iron Age and an art collection focusing on Funen artists), the Kulturhistorisk Museum (relics from medieval times), the DSB Railway Museum (historic rolling stock and model railway), and the Falck Museum (fire and rescue vehicles). The 19th-century Town Hall is a striking building with a modern

Hans Christian Andersen's birthplace, Odense

In Odense

wing containing works of art. Odense's cultural life features its own symphony orchestra and an excellent theatre. There is a Tivoli pleasure garden.

Several interesting places in the surroundings include the childhood home of the composer Carl Nielsen at **Nr. Lynd-else** (16km/10mi S). The **Ladby** Viking Ship (16km/10mi E) is a remarkable find, set in a field near a half-timbered farm overlooking the fjord. Its ancient timbers sunk into the earth, the ship was the final resting place of a chieftain from about 850. The grave had been plundered, but the anchor and chain are there, and you can see the bones of animals which accompanied the chieftain on his last journey. This site could be combined with a visit to the church of **Rynkeby** whose 400-year-old frescoes show angels playing 32 different instruments from those times. *Esbjerg 137km/85mi.*

Rudkøbing   O8
(pop. 4800) This is the main town on the long island of Langeland, linked by causeway and bridge to Tåsinge and Funen. There are many charming old houses and the Langeland Museum contains collections from prehistory as well as depicting urban and peasant life in the 18th and 19th centuries. **Tranekaer** (12km/7mi NE) is a lakeside manor house, rebuilt many times, in a lovely park open to visitors. From Rudkøbing there are ferry services to the island of Strynø and to Marstal on Aerø; and from Bagenkop in south Langeland to Kiel, Germany. *Esbjerg 195km/121mi.*

Svendborg   N8
(pop. 25,000) This is an excellent spring-

board from which to tour the lovely south Funen countryside (especially by bicycle) and island-studded Svendborgsund often alive with pleasure boats. Today commercial and industrial town, it is also very picturesque with its older districts of half-timbered warehouses, cobbled streets and pretty cottages. The town also has a Regional Museum and Romanesque St Nikolaj Church. To the south, Svendborg is linked by bridge to the wooded island of Tåsinge. Here is the pretty little town of **Troense** whose Maritime Museum is housed in a late 18th-century school and has a splendid collection of model ships. In the nearby Baroque Valdemar Castle is a Naval Museum. The church of **Bregninge** on the main road to Langeland harbours a fine head of Christ from about 1200 and there are lovely views from Kirkebakken (Church Hill) over the islands. *Esbjerg 178km/110mi.*

SEALAND
MØN, FALSTER, LOLLAND

Sealand's most distinctive attributes are Copenhagen, Roskilde, the concentration (especially in north Sealand) of imposing palaces and castles, and the all-important Sound, the control of which has been such a dominant factor in Danish history. This is the most industrial part of Denmark but there is still a lot of typical Danish countryside and coastline, with some of the most dramatic on the island of Møn.

Copenhagen see København

Frederikssund C7

(pop. 15,000) This modern industrial town at the narrowest point of Roskilde fjord developed from a fishing port whose ancient cottages can still be seen in the delightful Skyllebakke area near the harbour and shipyard. The J.F. Willumsen Museum is dedicated to the works of this great expressionist painter and sculptor. A major event is the Viking Festival (end June to early July), when local people recreate Viking life through plays based on Danish legends. The bridge across the fjord leads to the Hornsherred peninsula dotted with castles and churches, including **Jaegerspris**, a mansion mainly from the 16th–17th centuries, with royal memorabilia. *Copenhagen 40km/25mi.*

Helsingør/Elsinore B8

(pop. 55,000) This major seafaring and trading centre, with many ferry links to Helsingborg in Sweden across the narrow sound of Øresund, began its major development in the 15th century and much survives from its early days. The town centre is full of beautiful houses from the 16th–18th centuries, notably in Strandgade and Stengade streets. Famous Kronborg Castle, immortalized by Shakespeare in *Hamlet*, dominates the coast. It was built in the 16th century and rebuilt in its present Renaissance style after a fire in 1631. The interiors are splendid and include the uniquely preserved Chapel and huge Riddersalen (Knights' Hall). The

Danish Maritime Museum is also housed here. Among other major sights are the Cathedral of St Olai (built 1480–1559), beautifully preserved Gothic St Maria Church and Monastery (wonderful cloisters; Baroque organ still in use), the Town Museum and Carmelite Monastery, Marienlyst Slot (historical museum in former summer palace). Two very fine collections are those of the Technical Museum of Denmark (science and transport) and the Øresund Aquarium.

In summer, a veteran railway links Helsingør with **Gilleleje** (24km/15mi) on Sealand's north coast, passing through the major seaside resort and sailing centre of **Hornbaek** (12km/7mi; superb beaches,

Kronborg Castle, Elsinore

innumerable summer cottages). At **Humlebaek** (10km/6mi S) is the notable Louisiana centre of art and culture dedicated to modern Danish and foreign art and set in a lovely park overlooking the Sound. Nearby is a museum to the composer Niels W. Gade. *Copenhagen 47km/29mi.*

Hillerød   C8

(pop. 32,000) The town developed round Frederiksborg Castle, built in elaborate Dutch Renaissance style by Christian IV in 1600–20. After a fire in 1859, the castle was reconstructed according to the original plans, and has housed the National Historical Museum since 1878. The chapel, however, survived the fire; it is richly decorated with its altar and pulpit of ebony and silver, and a Compenius organ from 1610. This and the beautiful Knights' Hall head the list of Frederiksborg's considerable attractions, together with the magnificent Baroque gardens of the Castle Park. Other points of interest in Hillerød include the North Sealand Folk Museum in a charming 200-year-old thatched farm. At **Fredensborg** (9km/5mi NE) there is another castle. A gracious and more intimate building, used as the spring and autumn royal residence, Fredensborg Palace (Castle of Peace) was built in Italian style in 1722, following the Great Nordic War. The Park was created later in the 18th century on the lines of Versailles; one of its unusual features is Nordmandsdal, with 69 sandstone figures of Norwegian and Faroese fishermen in costume. From here it is only 15km/9mi NE to the most famous castle of all at Helsingør (above).

North west of Hillerød there are magnificent beaches by the pretty fishing hamlet of **Tisvildeleje** on Sealand's north coast. It is a distinctive landscape with attractive walks in Tisvilde Hegn, an area of shifting sands planted with woodland 200 years ago to halt erosion. The column of the Sand Drift Monument was erected at that time. A little inland is the 15th-century church of **Tibirke**, all that remains of a village engulfed by sand in the 18th century.
Copenhagen 36km/22mi.

Kalundborg   D5

(pop. 12,250) This industrial town on the west coast of Sealand has an important ferry harbour with services to Juelsminde and Århus in Jutland and to the island of Samsø. Its principal landmark is the massive 12th-century church with five towers. The town centre has a number of protected old buildings, one of which houses the museum. **Lerchenborg Castle** (5km/

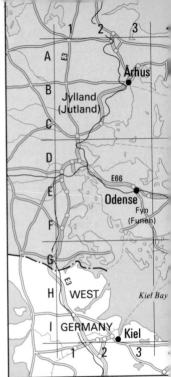

3mi S) is a Baroque manor house set in a fine park. Concerts and other events take place in its Rococo Knights' Hall.
Copenhagen 100km/62mi.

København/Copenhagen   D8

(pop. 1,500,000) Regular hydrofoils or ferries link the Danish capital with nearby Sweden, and ferries with Oslo. As well as being a great industrial and seafaring port, Copenhagen is one of Europe's most graceful cities with its myriad copper spires and domes punctuating the skyline above the narrow streets and canals of the old town or poking up out of the greenery of its many parks. Of the first castle, built by Bishop Absalon in 1167, only the foundations remain in the cellars of Christiansborg Palace, seat of the Folketinget (Parliament) rebuilt for the third time on the same site in 1907–28. Copenhagen became the capital in 1415, but much of its expansion and several of its finest buildings date from the reign (1588–1648) of the energetic Christian IV. It has had its share of siege and fires, and the majority of the oldest surviving buildings are from after the last

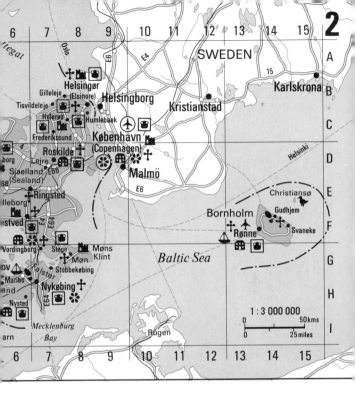

2

Baltic Sea

1 : 3 000 000

| 0 | | | 50kms |
| 0 | | 25 miles | |

reat fire of 1795. Bombardment by the nglish in 1807, during Denmark's liance with Napoleon, also caused much estruction. But there is still a great deal o see.

An efficient network of buses and elec-ric trains serve the centre and suburbs and an be freely used if you have bought a openhagen Card (see Tourist Cards, p. 8). There are also many daily sightseeing ours (various itineraries) round the city nd into the surroundings by bus, and also anal and harbour trips.

Your best first port of call is the Tourist nformation office at 22 H.C. Andersens oulevard, opposite the Town Hall; here ou can get a wealth of free literature, naps and a copy of *Copenhagen This Week* elling you what's on, where and when. If ou head north from here past Tussaud's Vax Museum, you come immediately into Rådhus Pladsen (Town Hall Square), ne of the principal hubs of the city rom which many sightseeing tours begin. t is dominated by the turn-of-the-entury Town Hall (famous Jens Olsen's World Clock) and the Lure Player Monu-

ment which is reputed to play every time a virgin passes!

Should you turn left from the square into Vesterbrogade you will very soon pass the entrance to far-famed Tivoli with its family entertainment from funfair thrills to sophis-ticated spectaculars and glorious gardens. Its ceremonial opening on May 1 marks the official beginning of summer. To the right, up Axeltorv, is another famous Copenhagen fun spot, the Circus. Just beyond Tivoli is the Central Railway Station and Air Terminal and ahead, across the road, you will see Den Permanente (modern Danish arts and crafts). Vesterbrogade soon leads to Vesterbrostorv and the Copenhagen City Museum (history, development and open air model).

Should you turn right across Rådhus Pladsen, you will enter Strøget, Copen-hagen's pedestrian-only shopping street, really a series of streets. It ends at Kongens Nytorv where you will find the Royal Theatre and Nyhavn, starting point for canal and harbour tours. About halfway along Strøget is the Church of the Holy Ghost (1730) bordering Gråbrodre-

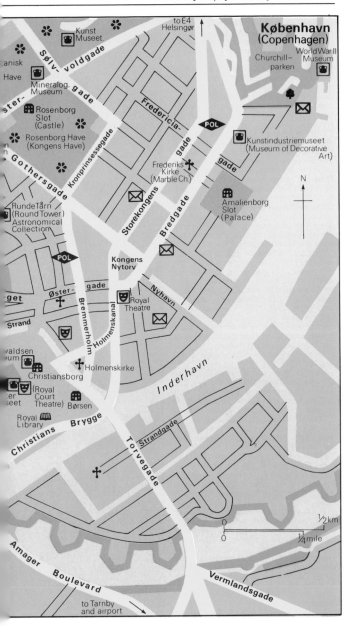

København (Copenhagen)

torv, a lively meeting place for the young, though the whole of Strøget presents an animated scene in summer, often with street musicians, theatres, protests, *etc*, in progress.

Many major sights can be reached by the narrow streets leading off Strøget. To the south you soon come to the attractive canal area of Gammel Strand. Across the canal is the Thorvaldsen Museum (dedicated to that great sculptor) and the massive complex of Christiansborg Palace, mentioned above, with adjacent Theatre History Museum in the Royal Court Theatre (1766) and Royal Stables (royal vehicles since 1778). Across the canal to the west is the 18th-century Prince's Palace housing the National Museum (fascinating collections ranging from prehistory to ethnography). East of Christiansborg, the Renaissance building on Christiansborg Castle Square with the distinctive dragons' tails spire is the Børsen (Stock Exchange), and across the canal the Renaissance Holmen's Church.

North of Strøget lie the neo-classical cathedral (1829), the main building of the university, the synagogue (consecrated 1833) and the Round Tower built in 1642 by Christian IV, its wide spiral ramp leading up to the Observatory and Astronomical Collection. Continue north and you soon pass the Baroque Reform Church and come to Rosenborg Castle, another creation of Christian IV and once the royal country residence; today it houses rich treasures including the crown jewels.

To the west are the fine Botanical Gardens, a few blocks to the east the Marble Church (completed 1894 with imposing exterior statues) and the royal residence of Amalienborg Palace (1749–60) with daily Changing of the Guard at 1200. It is only a few minutes walk north from here to Langelinie and the famous bronze statue (1913) of the Little Mermaid, pensively observing the ships that come and go. On the way you can pass the Medical History Museum, Museum of Decorative Art and the World War II Resistance Museum in Churchill Park.

For Copenhagen's other great focus of family fun, you take the suburban train north to **Klampenborg** where Durehavs-bakken (popularly known as 'Bakken'), Denmark's oldest amusement park, swings into action among the ancient oak trees in mid April. Adjoining it is the lovely Deer Park. To the west at nearby **Lyngby** is the excellent Open-Air Museum of Sorgenfri (old farms and houses, folk shows).

The city's night life is the liveliest and

(Background) Little Mermaid, Copenhagen

Royal Guard

Møns Klint

most varied in Scandinavia and its winter programmes range from music hall shows to the famous Royal Ballet. The big antique and art auctions are also fascinating; so are the several flea markets. For sights near Copenhagen, see **Helsingør, Hillerød, Frederikssund** and **Roskilde**. *Copenhagen–Esbjerg 278km/172mi.*

Maribo   H5
(pop. 5300) Attractively placed by the Maribo lakes in the heart of the island of Lolland, this little town grew up round the abbey of which the 15th-century cathedral is part. The lakes offer a pleasant recreational area for walking and boating. A short distance north and accessible by veteran railway from Maribo is Scandinavia's largest manor house park of **Knuthenborg** with a famous safari park crossed by 16km/10mi of road. **Nysted** (pop. 1500; 24km/15mi SE) developed round Ålholm Castle, one of Europe's oldest inhabited castles (originally 12th century); nearby is northern Europe's biggest Veteran and Vintage Car Museum. **Nakskov** (pop. 17,500; 27km/15mi W) is beautifully placed on its fjord and has some well-preserved houses and warehouses. St Nikolaj church is late Gothic. From **Tårs**, a little to the north west, there is a regular ferry service to Langeland.
Copenhagen 136km/88mi.

Møns Klint   G8
The beech-clad chalk cliffs on the east coast of the island of Møn offer one of the most startling landscapes in Denmark. They were formed 4000–5000 years ago but the high hill complex of Høje Møn, of which they are part, was created about 20,000 years ago. It is composed of layers of Cretaceous chalk moulded out of the primeval ooze 75 million years back and studded with marine fossils, and glacial deposits from the actions of the last Ice Age. A footpath at the edge of the forest leads to many exotic formations. To the north is the charming Empire-style chateau of Liselund in a splendid English garden. **Stege** (20km/12mi W) is the main community on Møn and has a medieval town gate (Mølleporten), Møn Museum and St Hans Church with distinctive late 15th century frescoes.
Copenhagen 123km/76mi.

Naestved   F6
(pop. 46,000) This town in south Sealand developed round religious foundations and later became a major port for the booming Hanseatic trade. It is linked by canal to the sea. Today an industrial and garrison town, it still retains many fine old buildings, including Denmark's largest Gothic church, St Peter's, which dates from the 13th–14th centuries. Naestved Museum

Roskilde Cathedral

in Helligåndshuset (1420) has a special section on leprosy. The important **Holmegård Glassworks** (8km/5mi NE), founded in 1825, can be visited. At **Sparresholm** (14km/8mi E), the stables of a 17th-century manor contain an interesting Carriage Museum. **Gavnø Castle** (7km/4mi SW) is a delightful Rococo creation with Denmark's largest privately owned art gallery and beautiful bulb gardens. *Copenhagen 82km/51mi.*

Nykøbing H7

(pop. 26,000) Principal town of Falster island, it is connected by bridge to the island of Lolland. The Gothic church is richly decorated and adjoins beautiful cloisters and monastery gardens with medicinal herbs. The District Museum is in a half-timbered house in which Peter the Great stayed in 1716. *Copenhagen 121km/75mi.*

Ringsted E7

(pop. 14,100) Situated in the centre of Sealand, this was an important town in medieval times. The brick Romanesque church of St Bendt was founded in the 12th century and contains the tomb of twelve medieval Danish kings. *Copenhagen 60km/37mi.*

Roskilde D7

(pop. 50,000) This has been a royal and episcopal residence since the 10th century. The cathedral, in Romanesque and Gothic styles, dates from the 1170s with later additions and houses dozens of Danish royal tombs, many of them magnificent works in marble and alabaster. Note that one of the figures at the foot of the sarcophagus of Christian IX in the chapel dedicated to him is of the same model as Copenhagen's Little Mermaid. There are also many memorial tablets, including beautiful examples of stonecutting from the Roskilde workshops from medieval times on. Connected to the cathedral by the 13th-century Absalon Arch is the Royal Mansion (1733). Roskilde's other great sights are to be found by the harbour in the Viking Ships Museum. Here you can see five remarkable vessels (dredged out of the fjord mud in 1962) which were deliberately sunk in the early 11th century to block enemy fleets approaching Roskilde, then an important trading town. Some of the vessels are still being painstakingly pieced together from the many thousands of pieces excavated from the sea.

Roskilde is a major centre for research and education and near **Lejre** (15km/9mi

Viking settlement, Trelleborg

SW) a most unusual piece of private research is in progress. Here at the Historical Archaeological Research Centre a scientific attempt to re-create conditions from the Iron Age is being carried out down to the last detail. This experiment in prehistoric living can be visited. In the same area the Baroque gardens of Ledreborg manor house (1744) are open to the public. Lejre village itself is an exquisite collection of half-timbered cottages. *Copenhagen 32km/19mi.*

Slagelse   E5

(pop. 33,000) This is a pleasant, busy commercial centre in the fertile region of west Sealand. Points of interest include St Mikkel Church in Gothic style and the ruins of Antvorskov monastery from the 12th century. An old church barn from the 16th century was at one time a grammar school, numbering Hans Christian Andersen among its pupils. **Trelleborg** (6km/4mi W) is one of the best-preserved Viking fortified circular encampments from the 11th century. The ground plan of the boat-shaped houses can be clearly seen and a full-size replica of one of them may be visited.
Copenhagen 89km/55mi.

Vordingborg   G7

(pop. 11,600) This manufacturing and garrison town in southernmost Sealand originally developed round the 12th-century castle of Valdemar the Great. The impressive castle ruins accommodate a Historical Botanical garden (medicinal, spice and ornamental plants) and include a 700m/2300ft ring wall as well as the Goose Tower, Denmark's best-preserved medieval fortress tower. The church has a fine three-aisled interior with frescoes. The bridge linking Sealand with the large island of Falster is over 3km/2mi long. *Copenhagen 92km/57mi.*

Bornholm   F14

(pop. 47,000) This Danish island in mid Baltic roughly halfway between south Sweden and Poland has its own special and varied character. You can reach it by air or by sea, with regular ferries from Copenhagen, and North German and Swedish ports. Its 567sq km/220sq mi offer something of everything: great beaches of fine sand in the south, high cliffs in the north, a verdant hinterland of farmland, forests and heathery hills, unspoilt little townships with crooked streets and half-timbered cottages, ruined castles, runic stones and fortified round churches. Smoked herring is the island's chief delicacy.

The main town is **Rønne** (pop. 15,000) on the west coast, partly rebuilt after Russian bombing in 1945. The old district

Christiansø

bund the church, opposite the yachting harbour, is charming. Note the Bornholm Museum, the Citadel on the town's southern outskirts and, 7km/4mi NE, the round church of **Nyker** with 14th-century frescoes. **Gudhjem** on the east coast is particularly pretty, its fig and mulberry trees and vines more reminiscent of the Mediterranean than the Baltic. From here a ferry serves the islet of **Christiansø** (50 mins), once a bastion of defence, now a magnet for seekers of peace, rare flora and varied bird life; other ferry services are from Sandvig/Allinge and Svaneke. The coast to the north of Gudhjem has the fabulous rock formations of **Hellig-doms-Klipperne** while inland the Rø Plantation offers lovely scenery. To the east of this, and a short distance south of Gudhjem, is **Østerlars** with Bornholm's

oldest and largest fortified round church (impressive 14th-century frescoes).

Svaneke, further south on the east coast, has won a European Council award for its beautifully preserved unity. In the southern hinterland **Åkirkeby**'s church is an impressive medieval building with twin saddle roof and fine 12th-century font. To the east is the wild rock and heather country of **Paradisbakkerne**. But some of the most dramatic sights of all lie on the coast north of Rønne: the soaring rock formations of **Jons Kapel**, for example, and the rugged and romantic ruins of medieval clifftop **Hammershus Castle** near Bornholm's northern tip.

The island has particular appeal for artists, walkers, cyclists and bird-watchers for whom there are good facilities and special packages.

Faroe Islands

FAROE ISLANDS

(The Faroes appear on Map 1, p. 33.) The 18 islands of the Faroes make up a self-governing region under the Danish kingdom. They cover an area of 1399sq km/540sq mi, have a population of 45,600 and lie roughly halfway between the Shetlands and Iceland. Originally discovered by Irish monks in the 8th century, they were colonized by Norsemen about 800 and adopted Christianity in 1000. In l035 they were attached to Norway and, with the latter, became united in due course with Denmark. When this union ended in 1814, the islands remained Danish; the present state of autonomy dates from 1948.

The Faroes' isolated position, buffeted often by the inclement moods of the North Atlantic, has contributed to the survival, unadulterated, of much of the islanders' cultural heritage. The Faroese language, for example, derives from ancient Norse and is most closely related to Icelandic. Their other great claims for attention are their spectacular coastal scenery, their remarkable bird life, some good angling and an unspoilt and uncomplicated way of life.

Only 6 per cent of the land is cultivated, the rest providing rough grazing for the sheep which outnumber the population by nearly two to one in winter and form an important part of the islanders' economy, clothing (woven or beautifully hand-knitted woollen goods) and diet. Much more significant, however, are the fisheries and the fish-processing industries which provide the overwhelming proportion of the Faroes' income. Mutton and fish, both air-dried and often eaten with unleavened bread, form a big part of the national diet. Guillemot and puffin meat are among local delicacies. So

is the whale meat acquired by the stric controlled but gory autumn cull that l brought the Faroes into unwelcome int national limelight in recent times. Alcoh other than light beer, is virtually impo sible to get on the islands.

The largest and most central island Streymoy and on it is the capital **Tórsha** (pop. 14,800). Here met the ancient Par ament on the hill of Tinganes from abc 900; today it is housed in attractive we preserved timber buildings. Sights inclu Skansin fortress (the present one da from the 1780s), the grass-roofed houses the older districts, and several museu devoted to Faroese archaeology, ethn graphy, natural history and seafari traditions.

Transport round the island is a combi ation of scheduled minibuses, taxis a ferries. The cliff scenery, in many plac rearing to 300–600m/1000–2000ft out the sea, with marine stacks and caves, enormously dramatic and some stretch carry tumultuous populations of puffi kittiwakes, guillemots, fulmars, gulls a shearwaters. Many species of duck a wader are to be found, too, among the the oystercatcher which is the Faroes' p tected national bird. Local advice shou be sought on the best areas and means getting to them.

As in Iceland, the landscapes of t Faroes have strong associations with ea sagas and their heroes, which give added dimension to the wild beauty. In number of places, old farms have been e cavated and, in some cases (*eg* at Saksun Streymoy) restored and equipped in eve detail to illustrate conditions from med eval times onwards. The Faroes' secor largest community is **Klaksvik** (pop. 460 on Bordoy, a lively centre for the activiti of the Faroese fishing fleets.

FINLAND

Finland's total land frontiers of 47km/1583mi, 538/335 are shared with Sweden, 733/456 with Norway and 76/793 with the USSR. Her 07km/688mi of coastline ranges from the Gulf of Bothnia in the west, the Baltic in the south west and Gulf of Finland in the south. The sea is broken up by tens of thousands of islands and skerries; the land fragmented by tens of thousands of lakes, and, in some regions, divided by long parallel lines of low ridges left by the retreat of the last Ice Age. Indeed, 9 per cent of the land is covered by inland waters, and this rises to 50 per cent in the great lake districts of the south east; over per cent is forest, the main agricultural areas being concentrated in the flat plains of the west. Dotted about these lake-and-forestscapes are the communities that have grown into townships, mostly originating as small industrial centres drawing their raw materials from the 'green gold' of the surrounding forests. The further north you travel the more sparsely scattered are the communities; but they are never lacking in modern buildings or the latest amenities, and some of the best examples of new architecture are to be found in the remotest places.

Ethnically, the Finns are the odd ones out in the Nordic countries. Except for the per cent who speak Swedish as their mother tongue, they belong to a different linguistic group (p. 30) and, acting as a buffer state between alien cultures over the centuries, they acquired influences from two directions. From Russia must have came the Orthodox faith which still has a substantial minority following, and such culinary items as *bortsch* (beetroot soup with sour cream), *blini* (pancake with smetana sour cream) and vodka (the Finns consider they produce the best). But by far the greatest influence came via the south west from Sweden, part of which Finland formed for about 600 years. This was the route taken by the dominant western church which resulted in the many medieval stone churches still to be seen in the south west today; and this was the route of the arts and manners of Europe, as well as a rather peaceful Reformation and, in due course, democracy.

Finland's huge and beautiful outdoors makes it a natural setting for open-air activities of all kinds. The Finns love to escape from their well-run cities at every opportunity and nearly all own or rent a summer cottage which can range from a simple hut to a minor mansion. Set in the heart of forests on river, lake or seashore,

it is an idyllic retreat from which to go boating, fishing, swimming, walking, picking berries, or just to contemplate from a granite boulder under a huge sky. You can do the same. This taste for simplicity is often combined with a profound interest in the literature, music and art of the world, which accounts for art centres in the heart of the countryside and a series of excellent cultural festivals punctuating the summer calendar (see gazetteer).

Probably the most famous Finnish speciality is the sauna (see also p. 23) which you will find in almost every hotel, hostel, campsite, holiday village and most private homes. The basic principle is one of dry heat which is why the body can withstand temperatures of 100°C/212°F and more. The heat comes from a stove in a corner of the sauna, nowadays usually heated electrically, but ideally by wood; this is topped by a pile of baking hot stones on which a small amount of water is thrown from time to time, adding moisture to the air and giving the illusion of a sharp rise in temperature. The best sauna is usually a small pine log cabin on a lake or seashore. The usual practice in a private sauna after sweating it out, is to wash and shower or plunge into sea or lake, then repeat the process as often as desired, usually rounding off with quiet relaxation and a cold drink on the balcony overlooking the water (in winter a hardy few roll in the snow or dip into a hole in the ice). Hotel or public saunas often impose a time limit, though there is sometimes a place to relax and take refreshment afterwards, an essential part of the process which is social as well as cleansing. In the old days, the sauna was usually built before the living quarters of a house, and it was considered a cure for almost all imaginable ills.

For communities with a substantial Swedish-speaking minority, the Swedish

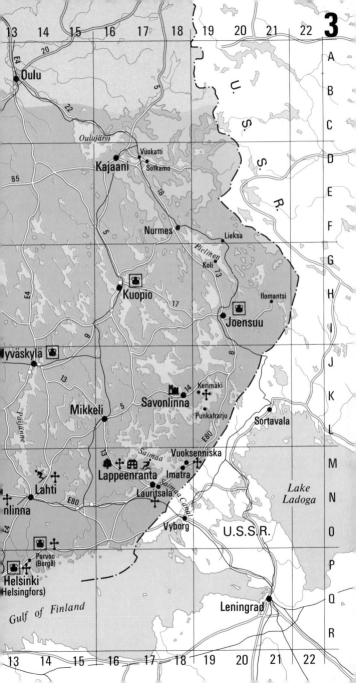

3

A
B
C
D
E
F
G
H
I
J
K
L
M
N
O
P
Q
R

13 14 15 16 17 18 19 20 21 22

E4
20
Oulu

22

U. S. S. R.

Oulujärvi

85

Vuokatti
Kajaani
Sotkamo

5

18

Nurmes

Lieksa

Pielinen

Koli

73

Kuopio

17

Ilomantsi

Joensuu

F4

9

6

Jyväskylä

13

Kerimäki

14
Savonlinna

Mikkeli

5

Punkaharju

Sortavala

E80

Päijänne

13

Saimaa

Vuoksenniska

Lappeenranta

Imatra

Lahti

Saimaa Canal

E80

Lauritsala

nlinna

F4

Vyborg

U.S.S.R.

Lake
Ladoga

Porvoo
(Borgå)

Helsinki
(Helsingfors)

Gulf of Finland

Leningrad

13 14 15 16 17 18 19 20 21 22

name is given after the Finnish in the following gazetteer. The exception is Åland, where the population is almost entirely Swedish-speaking and therefore the Finnish name is given after the Swedish.

SOUTH FINLAND

Åland Islands/ Ahvenanmaa   P5
(pop. 22,000) This scattering of over 6500 islands and skerries dotted about 10,000sq km/3860sq mi of sea makes up the autonomous province of Åland. 'Stepping stones' between Sweden and Finland, they were for a time a bone of contention between the two countries, but Finland's sovereignty was recognized by the League of Nations in 1921. The population, however, is almost entirely Swedish-speaking; they have their own flag, their own laws, and an ancient seafaring tradition which included some of the most famous sailing ships to travel the seven seas. Here are traces of countless prehistoric settlements, Viking graves and the remains of the oldest churches in Finland. Here, too, is an idyllic summer playground particularly well geared for sailing, other water sports and cycling and there is a wonderful rural calm to be enjoyed from a well-organized network of hotels, guest houses and self-catering cottages. Fishing and especially farming are main occupations, but Åland still has a merchant fleet out of all proportion to its size.

Mariehamn/Maarianhamina (pop. 9500) is the capital and the only town, a miniature garden city in summer with a profusion of flowers and leafy linden trees. It straddles a narrow peninsula, its main thoroughfares, Norra Esplanadgatan and Storagatan, linking the east and west harbours, about 2km/1mi apart. You can learn much about the archipelago – still growing at the rate of about ½m/2ft a century out of the sea – at the Ålands Museum. The Maritime Museum, West Harbour, has splendid displays of relics from famous windjammers; alongside is the museum ship, the four-masted barque *Pommern*.

Though the outer islands are rocky and rugged, the main island is extremely pretty, crisscrossed by narrow but well-surfaced lanes. The interesting restored castle of **Kastelholm** (25km/15mi NE of Mariehamn) was built by the Swedes in the 14th century, while the adjoining farm museum of Jan Karlsgården re-creates the islands' peasant culture. At **Bomarsund** (35km/21mi NE) are the ruins of a vast

naval fortress begun by the Russians a destroyed by Anglo-French forces in t Crimean War. Two of the finest mediev stone churches with wall paintings are **Jomala** (7km/4mi N) and **Finströ** (25km/15mi N). Other churches inclu **Hammarland** (21km/13mi NW **Eckerö** (37km/23mi NW), **Sund** (25k 15mi NE) and **Lemland** (13km/8mi SE The ruins of 13th-century **Lembö Chapel** enjoy a fine setting near one of t largest Viking cemeteries in the arch pelago. Numerous sea and air services li Åland with Sweden and mainla Finland.

Hämeenlinna   N1
(pop. 42,000) This small country tov was the birthplace of Jean Sibelius who childhood home is now one of seve museums. Modern buildings have r placed most of the wooden houses of t past, but the local castle is a wort medieval pile (restored) and can be vi ited. The most famous of several mediev greystone churches in the area is that **Hattula** (7km/4mi N), its interi entirely covered with early 16th-centu frescoes in excellent condition. **Aulan National Park** (3km/2mi N) is a fi civilized wilderness of artificial lakes a imported trees with a top-class hotel offe ing sports facilities. Hämeenlinna is t southern terminal of the popular Silv Line lake route (several hours) from Ta pere (p. 61). *Helsinki 104km/64mi.*

Hanko/Hangö   Q
(pop. 12,000) At the tip of a long peni sula on the Gulf of Finland, this is t best-known south-coast summer reso for bathing and especially sailin **Tammisaari/Ekenäs** (36km/22mi N is a charming little seaside town with ruined medieval castle of Raseborg in t vicinity. *Helsinki 126km/78mi.*

Helsinki/Helsingfors   P1
(pop. 500,000) Until 1812, Helsinki w an unimportant little market town ne the mouth of the River Vantaa. Ca Alexander I made it the new capital (s also Turku) and the present elegant d trict round the cathedral and South Ha bour, created by J.A. Ehrenström a Carl Ludvig Engel, dates largely from t 1830s. The main part of the city fills peninsula which is linked by bridge causeways and boat services to its wid spread suburbs and satellite towns. F even in the centre, the glint of the sea round almost every corner, and the na ral rock and trees are part of the urb scene.

Helsinki Guide and other free pub

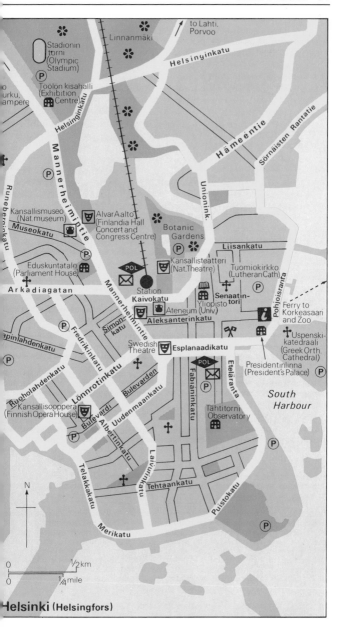

to Lahti, Porvoo

Linnanmäki

Helsinginkatu

Stadionin torni (Olympic Stadium)

Toolon kisahalli (Exhibition Centre)

Helsinginkatu

Hämeentie

Sörnäisten Rantatie

to urku, ampere

Mannerheimintie

Runeberginkatu

Kansallismuseo (Nat museum)
Museokatu

AlvarAalto (Finlandia Hall Concert and Congress Centre)

Botanic Gardens

Unioninkatu

Liisankatu

Eduskuntatalo (Parliament House)

Kansallisteatteri (Nat.Theatre)

Tuomiokirkko (LutheranCath.)

Pohjoisranta

Arkadiagatan

POL

Station

Mannerheimintie

Kaivokatu

Ateneum (Univ.)

Yliopisto (Univ.)

Senaatin-tori

Ferry to Korkeasaari and Zoo

apinlahdenkatu

Simon-katu

Aleksanterinkatu

Uspenski-katedraali (Greek Orth. Cathedral)

Fredrikinkatu

Swedish Theatre

Esplanaadikatu

Fabianinkatu

Eteläranta

POL

Presidentinlinna (President's Palace)

Ruoholahdenkatu

Lönnrotinkatu

Bulevarden

Kansallisooppera (Finnish Opera House)

Bulevardi

Albertinkatu

Uudenmaankatu

Tähtitorni Observatory

South Harbour

Telakkakatu

Laivurinkatu

Tehtaankatu

Puistokatu

N

Merikatu

0   ½km
0   ¼mile

Helsinki (Helsingfors)

Sibelius monument

(Background) Helsinki

cations give the latest details of what's on, when and where. Public transport is by tramcar, bus and the recently built metro system – a technological marvel probing deep into the city's granite foundations. The Helsinki Card gives unlimited use of these (see Tourist Cards, p. 28). An excellent route for orientation is the 3T tram, which describes a rough figure-of-eight through the city, bringing you back to your starting point.

You can pick this up by the South Harbour, which is high on the list of Helsinki's attractions, with its open-air morning market, all year and whatever the weather, selling fresh fish, flowers, fruit and vegetables as well as handicrafts and household goods. Regular and sightseeing boats set out from here to the islands, and several international shipping routes have their terminals here. Overlooking the harbour are the red-brick Uspenski Orthodox Cathedral, the President's Palace and Town Hall. Nearby, at Pohjoisesplanadi 19, is the City Tourist Office, from which a short side street leads to the elegant Senate Square dominated by the neo-classical architecture of the cathedral and other buildings.

The parklike boulevard, Esplanaadikatu, running west from the south Harbour, is where you find the displays and shops of several fashion and design firms. It ends at the Swedish Theatre on the main

artery of Mannerheimintie. Para with Esplanaadikatu to the north Aleksanterinkatu, linking the cathed with the commercial hub of the city a via side streets, with the main Railw Station and its square where you also f the National Theatre, the Ateneum Gallery, and the Central Post Office wh stands on the corner of Mannerheimin From here you can see the handsome c onnaded red-granite Parliament build and, further north, the churchlike tower the National Museum almost opposite imposing modern Finlandia Hall (Conc and Congress Centre by Alvar Aalto). F ther north still is the Olympic Stadi (fine view tower) and International F Centre (1975), a complex of exhibiti halls and well-planned open spaces.

Several main Helsinki sights are islands. There is Seurasaari with its op air museum of buildings from all over country, and summer theatre; Korkeass with its zoo; Suomenlinna, once cal the 'Gibraltar of the North', with its 18 century fortifications on a series of islan now a centre for leisure and the arts.

One of the gems of modern architect is Temppeliaukio Church, which was bu out of the living rock in the Töölö distri indeed modern architecture is an ov standing feature in all of greater Helsin with Tapiola Garden City as the m most famous example. Sightseeing tours

...e Saimaa

city, the suburbs and out-of-town des-
...ations begin from the bus station on
...onkatu. Recommended shorter trips
...to **Ainola** (home of Sibelius) and
...itträsk where the former home of three
...at architects is a charming lakeside
...seum and leisure centre, with near-
...Stone Age rock paintings. See also
...meenlinna and **Porvoo**.

...There is plenty of fairly expensive night
...e, open-air theatres and concerts, and
...nanmäki pleasure gardens is a fun
...ce for the family. The Helsinki Festival
...a major arts event in late August and
...ly September.

...ensuu   **I20**
...p. **45,000**) This pleasant provincial
...vn is one of the terminals of the Saimaa
...e fleet and mainly of interest as the
...teway to the unspoilt lake-and-forest
...untry of North Karelia. Karelia House
...ludes an interesting museum of the
...gion's culture. The **Koli Heights** (347m/
...38ft) are the highest point (75km/46mi
...above Lake Pielinen, with astounding
...ws over vast areas of waterlaced forests.
...ere are good hotel and self-catering
...ilities, and amenities for outdoor activ-
...s down by the lake. Regular boat ser-
...es on Pielinen link Joensuu, Lieksa,
...li and Nurmes in summer. **Nurmes**, at

the northern end of Pielinen (125km/77mi),
is a very pretty small town with many
wooden houses. East of Joensuu, **Ilomantsi**
(73km/45mi) is in the heart of the unspoilt
and predominantly Orthodox border
country with the Soviet Union and here a
strong folk tradition has survived. The
Pradznik or Praasniekka Orthodox Festivals are very colourful events at several
places in summer, especially at Ilomantsi
in mid July. *Helsinki 469km/291mi.*

Jyväskylä   J14
(pop. **63,000**) At the northern end of the
Päijänne lake system in central Finland,
Jyväskylä has a long tradition as an educational centre. Its university was designed
by Alvar Aalto. The Alvar Aalto Museum
and the Museum of Central Finland, with
handicrafts and workers' cottages, are the
most interesting collections. Just outside
the town is the important sports complex
centred on Laajavuori Hill. The forests to
the north are dotted with many holiday
villages offering hotels or self-catering
facilities and various outdoor activities.
The Jyväskylä Arts Festival is a major cultural event focusing on a different theme
each year (end June to early July). Regular
steamer services link Jyväskylä and Lahti
(below).
Helsinki 276km/171mi.

Lahti

Kajaani   D16

(pop. 34,000) The town's main attraction is as the doorway to the magnificently wild landscapes of Kainuu. It is built in the shelter of a now-ruined castle and was once Europe's greatest exporter of tar. It was while working here as a doctor that Elias Lönnrot collected the material that eventually became the Finnish national epic, *Kalevala* (p. 11). Eastwards lies a chain of lakes stretching to the Soviet border, with splendid facilities for outdoor activities, winter and summer, at **Sotkamo** (41km/25mi) and, near it, Vuokatti. *Helsinki 566km/351mi.*

Kuopio   H16

(pop. 75,000) This is the northern terminal for Saimaa lake traffic. From the tower on Puijo Hill the views are superb. The town has winding old narrow streets, a lively market and the collections in the Orthodox Church Museum are unique in western Europe. The Kuopio Dance and Music Festival is a lively event in June. *Helsinki 392km/243mi.*

Lahti   N14

(pop. 100,000) This modern city is best known as a ski centre and was the scene of the World Ski Championships in 1978. It lies between the two ridges of Salpausselkä on Vesijärvi, the southern end of the Päijänne lake system which links Lahti by boat services to Jyväskylä. The huge ski jump, modern architecture and sculptures are Lahti's main features, notably the Church of the Cross (Ristinkirkko) designed by Aalto in the town centre. In contrast, the old church and museum of **Hollola** (16km/10mi NW) are also interesting. An international Organ Festival begins in July. *Helsinki 103km/63mi.*

Lappeenranta   N

(pop. 54,000) Lappeenranta is the southern terminal for Saimaa lake traffic. There are also short cruises on the Finnish section of the **Saimaa Canal**, once an important commercial link with the Gulf of Finland. Since 1944 over half the canal has been in Soviet territory but, after long negotiations, it was restored and reopened in 1968. The town is a popular lake resort as well as a timber centre, with good facilities for excursions and water sports. Substantial remains survive of the fort and the entrenchments from the days when it was alternately a Finnish and a Russian garrison town, and these form part of a park with open-air summer theatre. Here, too, is the Orthodox Church (1785). The open-air market in the town centre is a lively spot. Two fine modern churches in the area are that of Taivaan Talo at **Lauritsala** (5km/3mi E) and the Church of Three Crosses by Alvar Aalto at **Vuoksenniska** near Imatra (37km/23mi NE). At **Imatra** the rapids of Imatrankoski were once one of the great natural beauties of Finland. Their power has been harnessed, but is released in full splendour on certain Sundays in summer.
Helsinki 221km/137mi.

Pietarsaari/Jakobstad

(pop. 20,500) This rather attractive small coastal town is an air and sea-traffic centre for connections across the northern Gulf of Bothnia to Sweden. Tobacco is the oldest of its several industries (there is a Tobacco

...stle at Savonlinna

...useum), but there are also strong cul-
...ral associations, notably with Finland's
...ational poet, J.L. Runeberg, born here in
...804. His school and his father's cottage are
...th museums. A scenic road leads through
...e archipelago to **Kokkola/Karleby**
...8km/23mi NE) a pleasant town of white-
...ashed houses. A curiosity is the English
...nding craft captured in the Crimean
...'ar, on display in English Park. **Kalajoki**
...02km/63mi N) is a place for beach ad-
...cts: a superb stretch of rolling dunes,
...ith varied accommodation and sports
...cilities. *Helsinki 500km/310mi.*

...ori **L8**
...op. 80,000) The sea has receded so that
...e major port of Pori at **Mäntyluoto** is
...w 20km/12mi NW from the centre of
...is modern industrial town. The Satakunta
...useum is one of the largest regional
...useums in Finland. The annual Inter-
...tional Jazz Festival takes place in July
... an island in the river. Near the port one
... the best beaches on the Baltic is Yyteri,
...w a tourist resort. Punctuating this
...retch of coast are some of Finland's
...ettiest towns in which districts of old
...ooden houses bordering leafy narrow
...reets still survive. They include **Rauma**
...0km/31mi S) and **Kristiinankaupunki/**
...ristinestad** (100km/62mi N). *Helsinki
...3km/150mi.*

...orvoo **P14**
...op. 20,000) The old part of the town is a
...cture-book place with brightly painted
...d wooden houses from the 16th-18th
...nturies. It is an important publishing
...ntre and has long attracted artists and
...riters. The 15th-century cathedral has in-

teresting frescoes, and a statue of Alexander
I is a reminder that here he appointed
Finland's first ever national legislative
assembly in 1809. The home of J.L.
Runeberg, Finland's natinal poet, is
among several museums; another is the
Art Museum devoted to 19th-century
sculptor Ville Valgren and painter Albert
Edelfelt. *Helsinki 50km/31mi.*

Savonlinna **K18**
(pop. 28,300) Situated in the very heart of
the Saimaa lake district, Savonlinna is a
timber centre and a holiday resort with
good facilities as well as being the hub of
regular boat services or cruises in every
direction. On summer mornings and evenings, the quayside is ever busy with the
comings and goings of lake traffic which
moors here overnight. The *Salama*, a ship-
wrecked schooner raised in 1971, is now a
museum to the long history of lake and
timber traffic. Olavinlinna, built in 1475 to
protect the shifting eastern frontier, is one
of the best medieval castles in Scandinavia,
and scene of an annual Opera Festival in
July (Festival Museum in restored villa).
The surrounding deeply forested countryside is beautiful, and the narrow ridge of
Punkaharju (30km/18mi SE) is a famous
beauty spot. Here Retretti is Finland's
largest art exhibition centre, including a
unique underground section. **Kerimäki**
(24km/15mi E) has Europe's largest wooden
church (1847).
Helsinki 334km/207mi.

Tampere/Tammerfors **L11**
(pop. 170,000) Finland's second city has
grown astride the rapids of Tammerkoski
on an isthmus between the big lakes of

Näsijärvi and Pyhäjärvi. Although it has a concentration of industry, Tampere is also a city of the theatre and the arts and its situation makes it a holiday centre in its own right. A Scotsman, James Finlayson, built the first cotton mill here in 1820, and it remains Finland's leading textile centre. Today a line of factories borders the tamed rapids, but green spaces are just as much a feature of the city. The biggest park is Pyynikki and its lakeside open-air theatre has the world's first revolving auditorium. Just across the isthmus in the park of Särkänniemi is a Recreation Centre dominated by Näsinneula Observation Tower (168m/550ft) which houses a planetarium, aquarium and children's zoo.

The city's excellent museums and art galleries include the Sara Hildén Art Museum (modern, highly imaginative), the Häme Museum (excellent regional collection), the Technical Museum (all types of vehicles over the centuries), a charming Doll Museum at Kaukajärvi (5km/3mi), and the Lenin Museum (it was here that Lenin and Stalin first met). The cathedral in National Romantic style (1902–7, Sonck) has some famous paintings, among them Hugo Simberg's macabre *Garden of Death*. In contrast, Kaleva Church (1966, Pietilä) is distinctively modern, while the surrounding countryside has a number of well-preserved medieval stone churches, including that of **Messukylä** (5km/3mi SE). The city has many fine sculptures, notably by Wäinö Aaltonen (traditional) and Eila Hiltunen (modern). The annual Tampere Theatre Summer occurs in August. Tampere is the northern terminal for the Silver Line lake route from Hämeenlinna (p. 56), and southern terminal for the Poet's Way boat tour to Virrat (7½ hours). *Helsinki 176km/110mi.*

Turku/Åbo   O8

(pop. 165,000) See also Tourist Cards (p. 28). This is Finland's most ancient city and was her capital until 1812 when Czar Alexander I considered it too far from St Petersburg for security and chose Helsinki instead. It is still a major administrative and educational centre, and is Finland's most important year-round ice-free port with many sea and air links to Sweden. There are two universities, one teaching in Finnish, one in Swedish; the former is a striking example of modern architecture. It is a restful city, with the River Aura winding through the centre fringed by little boats and bordered by parks whose trees frame the distinctive single tower of the cathedral. This is one of Turku's three most famous sights, originally completed at the end of the 13th century, but damaged, restored or extended over the

centuries. Many notable historical fig are buried here. The two other m sights are the medieval but restored ca close to the harbour, housing a fine torical Museum; and the Luostarinn Handicraft Museum, a street of old ho that survived the great fire of 1827, no charming open-air museum peopled summer with craftsmen demonstra their skills.

Many of the older districts of Tu have been rebuilt; some of the more st ing modern buildings along the river clude the City Theatre, the Wäinö Aalto Museum (partly devoted to Finland's n famous sculptor) and the Sibelius Muse There is a lively morning market on the square of Kauppatori, and a second-h market in Aninkaistentori. Two not modern churches are the Resurrec Chapel (1941, Bryggman) and Chapel the Holy Cross (1967, Pitkänen). **Ruiss** 10km/6mi W of the city, is a lovely p with golf and other sports facilities.

Between Turku and the Åland isla (p. 56), thousands more islands and sker rise out of the sea, some linked by a se of bridges, causeways and ferries, oth by boat services, to the mainland, prov ing a wide variety of excursions. The r to **Korpoo**, necessitating several ferries one recommendation. Seven medie churches in Turku's surrounding coun side offer the theme of another tour. small towns of **Naantali** (16km/10mi N with its 15th-century Convent Church the presidential summer residence,

Naantali Bridge

Uusikaupunki (78km/48mi NW) are pecially picturesque. The annual Tu Music Festival takes place in Augu *Helsinki 167km/104mi.*

Vaasa/Vasa

(pop. 54,000) This is the main west-c centre for sea and air connections acr the Gulf of Bothnia to Sweden. It was headquarters of the White Guards in War of Independence against the R Guards in 1918. After a devastating fire 1852, the new town was moved closer the receding sea; remains of old Va

...rches, castle, a museum) can be seen ...the original site at Mustasaari. In the ...dern town, the Ostrobothnian Museum ...good regional collections and the Brage ...en-Air Museum at Hietalahti is a collec-...of old farm buildings. There are also ...ghtful island trips by waterbus. *Helsinki ...km/257mi.*

NORTH FINLAND

...s section deals mainly with the northern-...st province of Lappi (Finnish Lapland) ...etching from just south of the Arctic ...cle almost to the Arctic Ocean, but it ...includes the northern city of Oulu and ...fell district of Rukatunturi, both of ...ich lie outside the boundaries of Lappi. ...Until World War II, much of it was a ...ckless wilderness, but war brought new ...ds, armies and eventually devastation. ...ch of the area was destroyed by retreat-...German armies in 1944. Since then ...phisticated pockets of civilization have ...ltiplied and roads have probed ever fur-...er into the forests and tundra. Yet, ...ough the region is now easily accessible ...d offers every modern comfort, silent ...meval landscapes wait unchanged just ...nd the corner for those willing and ...uipped to enjoy them. Forests, swamps, ...ift streams and bare-headed fells are the ...ief characteristics of these landscapes, ...s countless lakes some of which are im-...nse. The trees become more and more ...nted as latitude and altitude increase. ...entually conifers are left behind and ...en forests of dwarf birch finally give way ...the miniscule vegetation of the tundra. ...Economically, Lappi is a poor province. ...ere is some light industry in the south, ...t the economy is mainly based on for-...ry and reindeer breeding. Most of the ...ar, the reindeer roam free, but they are ...unted, marked or slaughtered once a year ...colourful reindeer roundups, usually ...late autumn and winter when zipping ...soes and pounding hooves conjure up a ...ild West film in an Arctic setting. But ...u need to check 'when' and 'where' on ...e spot. Of Lappi's 200,000 inhabitants, ...ly about 3500 are Lapps – or Same (pro-...unced Saa-me), as these proud people ...efer to be called (see also pp. 91, 118). ...w now wear the bright traditional cos-...mes, except on special occasions such ...church festivals; and only a very few ...milies follow the reindeer herds on ...asonal migration. Most have settled in ...all homesteads, many have taken up a ...de or profession, and the youngsters

mostly indulge in the same tastes and pursuits as youngsters elsewhere. Note that the Same people of northern Finland include a small group with quite different cultural features. They are the Skolt Lapps who historically were influenced by the Russians and other peoples to the east; they follow the Orthodox faith and have their own traditions. Most live in the Ivalo area or in the remote village of Sevettijärvi in the north east.

Two main roads and a network of minor ones, most of them served by regular bus, send their threads across the Lappi map. Air services reach to Kittilä in the west and, daily to Ivalo in the far north. The best way to experience Lappi is to choose one or two centres and then walk – you will learn nothing from a few days speeding along its roads. But you should never venture alone in the wilderness unless you are experienced, and always tell someone where you are going and when you expect to be back. In summer be prepared for large numbers of mosquitoes, though some years are worse than others.

Spring (late May–June), following the retreat of a long, tough winter, is an exhilarating time to visit Lappi; in autumn (from early September) the colours are so spectacular that the Finns have a special word for it: *ruskaa.* There is superb cross-country skiing in winter and early spring, the latter's lengthening days and clear air producing enviable suntans. The shifting coloured veils of the Northern Lights sweeping the sky in the darker months are quite unforgettable.

Enontekiö   F5

One of the most attractive of the Lappi church villages, Enontekiö (old name Hetta) is scattered along the northern shore of narrow Ounasjärvi lake from whose southern shore rise the Ounastunturi fells crossed by a marked hiking trail (p. 66). It lies 26km/16mi east of highway 21 and also has road links northwards with Norway. As the main village for an enormous area, its attractive modern church and other amenities serve scattered communities of the Same people. *Rovaniemi 315km/195mi.*

Inari E9

This community on the south-west shore of huge Lake Inari is an important centre for the Same people from a wide area, and colourful weddings and sports events take place here, usually at Easter or Lady Day. There are also many winter reindeer roundups in the surrounding wilderness. In summer, excursions on the island-studded lake, fishing and hiking are the main attractions. There is an interesting Same Museum in the village from which a marked trail (15km/9mi return) leads to a remote 18th-century wooden church at Pielppäjärvi. Other marked hiking trails start from **Njurgalahti** (46km/28mi SW), a Same community in the Lemmenjoki river goldwashing area, and some guided trips are arranged.
Rovaniemi 335km/209mi.

Lapp, Lake Inari

Ivalo E10

On the banks of Ivalojoki river and astride highway 4, this large village is a main traffic and trading centre for northern Lappi, with Finland's northernmost airport. Its proximity to Inari and the extensive and wild **Saariselkä** fells are its main tourist attractions. The latter lie to the south of Ivalo and east of highway 4, and are serviced by a number of tourist centres near the main road; there is a number of marked hiking trails. A minority Same group, the Skolt Lapps (p. 63), live in the Ivalo area.
Rovaniemi 295km/183mi.

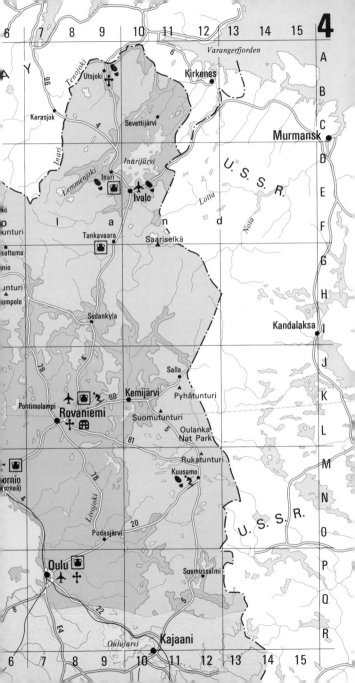

Kilpisjärvi   D2

Near the tip of the north-western arm of Finland, Kilpisjärvi and its lake lie close to the border with Sweden and Norway. Indeed, the boundary stone where the three countries meet, to the north west, is a popular destination for walkers, 24km/15mi from the village. A marked trail leads to it via Malla Nature Reserve with its varied and protected flora (permit needed, available from the excursion centre or tourist hotel); or you can do most of the journey by boat across the lake. The village is dominated by Saana fell (1029m/3375ft) once considered holy by the Same people; the very easy climb is rewarded by superb views. Beyond it, the roadless wilderness merges into Norway and includes Finland's highest fell, Haltia (1328m/4356ft). *Rovaniemi 440km/273mi.*

Kuusamo   M12

Kuusamo, on highway 5, is the nearest village to the splendid **Rukatunturi** fell district (25km/15mi N). Here you will find varied accommodation in a magnificently wild setting, and amenities for summer hiking and winter skiing. The popular marked trail known as the Bear Circuit (55km/34mi, but shorter variations possible) links Rukatunturi with Kiutaköngas to the north across the high forested hills of Oulanka National Park, ribbed by deep valleys and racing rivers. From Rukatunturi you can also shoot the rapids with an expert through a nearby canyon. *Helsinki 833km/517mi, Rovaniemi 195km/121mi.*

Oulu   P7

(pop. 95,000) This lively northern city was one of the world's most important tar export harbours in the 19th century; today it concentrates on timber, paper and chemical products. Oulu grew round the Merikoski rapids whose waters feed the big power station designed by Alvar Aalto. The busy riverside Market Square is overlooked by the city's ultramodern theatre and a contrasting group of ancient salt storehouses. Other points of interest include the cathedral (1845, Engel), the North Ostrobothnian Museum in Ainola Park and the open-air Museum on Turkansaari, an island in the river (13km/8mi E). *Helsinki 617km/382mi.*

Pallastunturi   F5

The tourist complex here takes its name from a group of 14 fells and lies 31km/19mi E of Muonio on highway 79. It is magnificent fell-walking (and skiing) country with a marked hiking trail from the hotel over the Pallastunturi and Ounastunturi fells to Enontekiö (64km/

40mi N; p. 63). In some of the small co munities such as **Raattama** and **Ylik** very old wooden houses survived war struction because of their remoteness, are now accessible by a minor road wl provides an attractive alternative rout Enontekiö. *Rovaniemi 260km/161mi.*

Rovaniemi

(pop. 30,000) Rovaniemi was almost to destroyed by the retreating German arm 1944, and was rebuilt according to pl by Alvar Aalto. It stands at the junctio the Kemi and Ounas rivers, only a miles south of the Arctic Circle. modern architecture and amenities of administrative capital of the province Lappi come as a surprise to those exp ing a backwoods town. It has excel hotels, varied shops and is the gate for air and road traffic throughout La Lappia House is the civic centre comp designed by Aalto, housing the thea concert hall, and the Lapland Provin Museum. A little outside town are Ethnographic and Forestry Museums Pöykkölä. The modern parish church h huge altar fresco *The Source of Life* Segerstråle). Rising out of the town are Ounasvaara hills which give their nam the annual international ski championsh in March. The Arctic Circle 'village' (8) 5mi) features the workshops (and sho) of Santa Claus and a small museum North Polar exploration. **Pohtimolar** Sports and Excursion Centre (28km/1' NW) has the world's only reindeer driv school. *Helsinki 850km/528mi.*

Tankavaara

A short distance from highway 4 lies unusual museum run by the associatior gold prospectors in Finnish Lapland. I a 'gold village' reconstructed by a stre in the forests, and combines the hist of over a century of goldwashing in province with the opportunity to pan gold yourself under expert guidan Self-catering accommodation is availa *Rovaniemi 230km/142mi.*

Tornio/Torneå   N

(pop. 22,000) At the northernmost end the Gulf of Bothnia, Tornio is a bor town, facing Sweden's Haparanda (p. 1 across the River Tornio. Its port is 10l 6mi from the town. Quite a few ol buildings remain in this peaceful prov cial town which has been a trading cer since the 14th century; they include wooden church (1686). The Tornio Va Museum is worth visiting, especially if y are planning to travel north through landscape fed by this bor

...kaa, *near Utsjoki*

...er with Sweden. *Helsinki 760km/*
...2mi.

...tsjoki   **B9**
...is thinly scattered community, close to
... northern border with Norway, is a
...jor Same centre near the confluence of
... Utsjoki and Tenojoki rivers (famous
...mon fishing). A road now follows the
...rder south along the Tenojoki and
...arijoki rivers through very remote wil-
...rness country to Angeli. The church
...60) is one of the few in Lappi to have
...rvived World War II. There is good
...hing in the rivers and hiking across
...ndra and through forests of dwarf birch.
...aniemi 467km/289mi.

ICELAND

Far flung out to sea, Iceland straddles the
Mid-Atlantic Ridge, a 20,000km/
12,000mi section of submarine mountain
ranges created by the upheavals of the
earth's crust many millions of years ago.
As the continents of America and Europe
slowly creep further apart, the Atlantic
Ocean floor widens at the rate of about
2½cm/1in a year and, along with it, Iceland
widens too. The oldest rocks yet dated are
only about 16 million years old. It is a
young land, still in the making, and there
are few other places where you are more
aware of nature's immutable forces.

Of Iceland's area of 103,300sq km/ 39,750sq mi, only about a quarter is habitable, mostly in the coastal areas and in some of the broad valleys running down to the coast from the highlands. The rest of the country is made up of glaciers, volcanoes and their attendant expanses of lava, other non-volcanic mountains, hot springs, sand and gravel deserts and large stretches of stony wilderness. All of Iceland is liberally laced with waterways ranging from rushing rivers and chattering streams to numerous lakes.

Glaciers cover $11\frac{1}{2}$ per cent of the country, the largest of them, Vatnajökull, is a sprawling white mass of 8400sq km/3240sq mi, as big as all the glaciers of continental Europe put together. In thickness, it reaches an impressive 1000m/3280ft, and one of its outlets extends to about 120m/400ft below sea level. In the south of this massif is Iceland's highest point, Öraefajökull (2119m/6950ft). Four other mighty glaciers are Langjökull and Hofsjökull in the Central Highlands, Mýrdalsjökull in the south, and Drangajökull in the north west. There are numerous smaller ones too, so that you are rarely without an ice cap on or just over the horizon.

Science fiction landscapes form the backdrop to a deep-rooted Icelandic culture which flourished in the farms and small communities from early medieval times and survives in the sagas and other early Icelandic literature, and in the Althing (Parliament), one of the world's oldest democratic legislative bodies.

Many of the forces of nature have been harnessed to provide power and heating for the needs of modern society and to inject a much-needed diversification into the national economy which, until recent years, was based almost entirely on fishing and its by-products. Today, Iceland has energy for sale and an increasing number of foreign investors are interested in purchasing this precious commodity. The country's (pop. 240,000) earlier massive rate of inflation has been reduced to 10%.

A few years ago, a road was built along the south-east coast at the foot of Vatnajökull massif and this remarkable engineering feat completed the route round the whole of Iceland. The principal sights are listed in the following sections on North and South Iceland, but it is strongly recommended, if you have the time, to take one of the many organized tours into the uninhabited interior. These usually take the form of camping trips with tents and all meals provided. Sturdy vehicles are used over the extremely rough tracks that penetrate landscapes of the utmost wild magnificence. If you have a

special interest in birds, plants or geo you will be particularly well served.

Akureyri and the North

(pop. 12,500) The principal town of no ern Iceland, Akureyri is a pleasant un, tentious place with a fine situation on mountainous shoreline of Eyjafjör about 60km/37mi from the open sea. most dominant building is the chu completed in 1940 and reached by steps from the town centre. There several museums of local interest and Iceland's best botanical gardens contain over 2000 species and varieties from over the world. This quiet little t periodically bursts into life when a cr ship calls or summer coachloads of visi arrive. A short drive away on the slope Hlidarfjall is Iceland's main ski hotel.

About 100km/62mi east is the n famous area in northern Iceland: Mýva a lake with such an extraordinary g logical setting and richness of bird (perhaps the world's largest concentra of breeding duck) that it acts as a ma for ornithologists and geologists the wo over. The lake covers 38sq km/15sq and lies at the heart of a once very ac volcanic area on a plateau about 30 1000ft high. There is a road all the round it. A curious feature is the li church at Reykjahlíd, which, though vi ally surrounded by lava, stands untouc in a small clearing. Near Reykjahlíd bleak lava field is rent by a profound sure and here there are caves contain the hot water bathing pools of Stóragjá Grjótagjá. Even stranger is the lava fiel Dimmuborgir (black castles), a tormen landscape which was created about 2 years ago on the east shore of the lake; ta great care not to get lost. Just a few m east of Rekjahíd are the pale, parc

...reyri

...s of Námaskard and, on the plain be-
..., bubbling pits of blue, grey or red
...d, clear pools, all steaming and hissing
...essantly amid warning notices in several
...guages telling you to be very wary of
...ere you tread.

...urther east you reach the canyon of the
...cial river Jökulsá á Fjöllum thundering
...wn from distant Vatnajökull towards the
...th coast; on the way if forms Europe's
...ghtiest waterfall, **Dettifoss**. Such is the
...ce of water that the canyon is being
...gthened at the rate of 1m/3ft per year.
...e sight and sound are staggering. A little
...the north is **Åsbyrgi National Park**,
...tly composed of the former bed of the
...yon before the river changed course;
...lushness and variety of the vegetation
...quite startling, as is the fantastic geo-
...ical architecture of Hjódaklettar, a sec-
...n of the park where cliffs and towers of
...k have been torn and twisted by forces
...unimaginable power. Nearby on this
...rthern coast at **Tjörnes** are the fascinat-
...crumbling cliffs composed of fossilized
...lluscs and plants ranging in age from
...eral thousand to several million years.
...ese cliffs include evidence of creatures
...nd only in the Pacific. To the south is

the attractively placed little fishing town of
Húsavík with views out to the island of
Grímsey. This northernmost fragment
of Iceland, which actually straddles the
Arctic Circle, can be visited by air, boat or
hydrofoil from Akureyri.

The rugged Austfirdir (eastern fjords)
lie a little over 300km/188mi east of
Akureyri. The small but important port of
Seydisfjördur is the main centre and, a little
inland, **Egilsstadir**, by the long lake of
Lagarfljót, is well placed for exploring the
area. The lake is fed by the icy waters flowing down from Vatnajökull and is said to
harbour a monster. At **Hallormstadur**, on
its eastern shore, one of Iceland's few forests
(and its largest) is the result of experimental
re-afforestation earlier this century.

The north-west coast of Iceland is made
up of the great clawlike peninsula of
Vestfirdir (western fjords), a mainly wild
region of deep fjords, sheer cliffs and basalt
rock. **Isafjördur** (pop. 3000) is the main
community, depending mainly on fishing
and the fish-processing industries. From
here the scheduled boat service, calling at
small communities all around the deeply in-
dented fjord system, also provides a memorable full-day excursion.

Reykjavík and the South H4

(pop. 85,000) Reykjavík, the Icelandic capital, means 'smoke bay': a combination of the many thermal springs in the area and the fine natural harbour; it is actually a completely smokeless city. It developed from a small community at the turn of the century and even now gives the impression of a toy town, with its neat streets of red, blue, green and yellow houses, many built of corrugated iron, bordered by lava fields, pastures and the sea, and overlooked by Esja mountain (909m/2982ft). From the observation platform at the top of Hallgríms church tower you get a good idea of the layout. In front of the church is the imposing statue of Leifur Eiriksson who discovered North America.

The city centre is near the harbour, with the greystone Parliament (Althing, 1881) next to the slightly older little cathedral on Austurvöllur square, near the main post office. This district is separated from the newer business and shopping areas by Laekjargata, at the northern end of which is the grassy mound of Arnarhóll, sheltering the cosy building that houses the offices of the President and Prime Minister, and the statue of Ingólfur Arnarson, Iceland's first settler. Near here, on Laekjartorg, there is the tourist information tower. Arnarhóll is also the focal point for national celebrations. The southern end of Laekjargata brings you to Tjörnin, a large and delightfully rural pond on which there is always a varied collection of ducks and seabirds waiting to be fed. South of this is the National Museum and Art Gallery, the university, ultramodern Nordic House (cultural exhibitions) and the Árni Magnússon Manuscript Museum harbouring a unique collection of ancient manuscripts, including some of the ancient sagas. Nearby are the expanses of domestic Reykjavík Airport; the international airport is at Keflavík (50km/31mi W).

The most charming of Reykjavík's museums is Árbaer Folk Museum on the eastern outskirts, comprising a collection of rare old buildings. Otherwise there are several worthwhile galleries for those interested in art and sculpture, among them Kjarvalsstadir, Ásgrímur Jónsson Art Gallery, Einar Jónsson gallery and the sculptures of Ásmundur Sveinsson. A summer show in English, called 'Light Nights', gives a pleasant introduction to Icelandic traditional tales and folk songs.

There are organized sightseeing tours of the city and many half- and full-day excursions in summer into the countryside of south-west Iceland where many of the main sights are concentrated. Several them are usually combined in one tour.

To the east of Reykjavík is Thingve (50km/31mi) where, in a setting of gr drama, the Icelandic national assem met against a backdrop of volcanic c from about 930. Laugarvatn (75km/4(E) is a popular lake in a wild setting, wi riding centre. Gullfoss (122km/76mi E one of Europe's greatest waterfalls an spectacular sight. Geysir (116km/72mi has given its name to hot springs and wa heaters all over the world; the origi Great Geysir tends to be lazy these da but nearby Strokkur spews out a mig water spout at intervals of a few minu The surrounding area is a bubbling ca dron of mud of many colours and cry clear pools. At Skálholt (92km/57mi E the Christian heart of the country on wh a church has stood for nine centuries; present exquisitely simple building da from only 1963. Finally there is Hverage (46km/28mi SE) famous for the springs that feed its greenhouses and n there is also a well-equipped Nature C Sanatorium.

Arctic Circle

A Ísafjördur Dra

Ísafjördur

B

C

D Breidhafjördhur

E Stykkishólmur

Snaefellsjökull Snaefellsn

F Arnarstapi

Faxaflói

G Hva

Reykja

H Keflavík

I

1 2 3

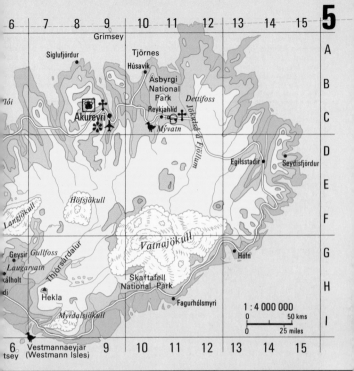

The following destinations are further
afield and preferably require at least two
days. The **Snaefellsnes** peninsula, about
250km/155mi north of Reykjavík, points a
massive finger out into the Atlantic and has
very strong associations with both the fact
and fiction of the sagas, especially Laxdaela
saga and Eyrbyggia saga. It was also from
its coast, just east of the busy little fishing
port of **Stykkishólmur**, that Eirikur
raudi (Eric the Red), outlawed for some
times, set sail and discovered Greenland.
Snaefellsnes is topped by the ice cap of
Snaefellsjökull from whose central crater
began Jules Verne's 19th-century novel
Journey to the Centre of the Earth. Modern
ascents of this distinctive mountain
(1446m/4730ft) can begin close to the fishing village of **Arnarstapi**, but it is advisable to have a guide. The peninsula, incidentally, also has some of the most varied
and colourful geological formations in
the country.

About 135km/84mi south east of
Reykjavík is **Thjórsárdalur**, Iceland's
largest river valley, overlooked by one of
the most famous and restless landmarks,

volcanic **Hekla** (1491m/4891ft) which has
erupted several times in recent years. It
dominates a wild, sparsely inhabited area
which, in saga times, prior to a major eruption in 1104, was fertile farmland. Dating
from that period is the farm of **Stöng**, now
restored and well worth visiting for itself
and its setting.

One of the most exciting trips of all is via
the remarkable and recently completed
road along the south-east coast to **Höfn**
(484km/301mi) which is becoming something of a tourist centre. The road passes
by **Skaftafell National Park**, a magnificent area at the southern fringes of the
Vatnajökull massif, beneath Öraefajökull.
The contrasts between vivid green vegetation, deserts of black sand, white glaciers
and the waters streaming from them to the
sea are unforgettable. From Höfn there are
also glacier trips on to outlying areas of
Vatnajökull, or you can head north to
Austfirdir (eastern fjords; p. 69).

Day trips and longer stays are arranged
from Reykjavík to the **Westmann Isles**
(Vestmannaeyjar) off the south coast,
where the mighty eruption of Helgafjell

(Holy Mountain) in 1973 partially buried the little town of **Heimaey** and caused the urgent evacuation of the entire population of about 5300. Now rebuilt, this unusual place, literally risen from the ashes, makes a lasting impression. An unexpected benefit, likely to be available for the next 50 years, is the unlimited hot water supply achieved by pumping cold water into lava. The islands are also known for egg-collectors who swing from ledge ledge down vertical cliffs. The seabird is rich indeed. A short distance from Westmann Isles is **Surtsey** another canic product, born in 1963. Acces limited to scientists.

Gullfoss waterfall

Mount Hekla

Strokkur

(Background) Black castle near Mývatn

NORWAY

enically, Norway is one of the most amatic countries in the world. Surunded on three sides by sea, its coastline about 3300km/2100mi stretches to ,400km/16,400mi – or over half the circumference of the earth – when you clude the astonishing complexity of its dentations and larger islands. Its land ontiers consist of 1619km/1005mi ared with Sweden, 716km/444mi with nland, and 196km/122mi with the viet Union. It is largely composed of gh plateaus intersected in the south east deep valleys and in the west by labyrinine fjords. More than half its surface is er 600m/2000ft high, much of it of a solate magnificence; the highest point, littertinden, in the Jotunheim range, is 72m/8110ft. All this, contained within a area of 320,000sq km/123,500sq mi, is ared by a population of little over 4 illion.

Some of Scandinavian man's earliest aces (notably rock carvings) are in Norway. In the Middle Ages, following the lonizing escapades of the Norwegian kings, Norway's territory was more an twice its present size, and outposts cluded Iceland, Greenland and fragents of Britain. Many of the most teresting sights have their origins in ose times. Later, many overseas possesons were ceded to Denmark and, until dependence was declared in 1905, orway's political fortunes were closely, d often uncomfortably, linked first with enmark and, in the 19th century, with weden.

Most of the population, however, has ruggle so hard for a livelihood in remote lleys and fjords, that what went on yond their particular mountain was of ademic importance. Many excellent en-air museums illustrate this past way life. It could take weeks to reach the arest town, involving arduous journeys horse and/or boat. Out of such journys came the first simple staging posts for st and worship; some of Norway's most nous hotels and interesting churches veloped from these humble origins. emoteness bred a high degree of selfficiency and gave rise to many of the ills and art forms which survive today; e timber-built stave churches, for exple, of which about 25 survive from the th or 13th century, are unique to orway. The beautiful rustic art of rose inting, which reached its peak in the late th and early 19th centuries and embelhes interiors and furniture in several gions, has many local variations. The

rose, incidentally, is only one motif of this art form which also includes geometric patterns, figures and even landscapes. Folk music, ballads and dancing have their roots in early medieval times, and trolls, battles and other heroic deeds are recurrent themes. Later influences came from mercenaries returning from the war in Poland around 1600, and the 'polsdans' evolved into a special Norse folk dance – a hybrid of old and new with many regional variations.

In due course, tracks became lanes and, by dint of remarkable engineering feats, main roads and railways bored through apparently impenetrable terrain. Almost any journey in Norway would qualify as scenic elsewhere, and many are utterly breathtaking. Even for those without a car, the complex network of air, bus, rail, ferry and hydrofoil services operating (mostly) like clockwork, make it possible to visit the remotest areas with ease, though not necessarily with speed. Walkers will find unparalleled opportunities for expending their energy, especially by taking advantage of the unique facilities of the Norwegian Mountain Touring Club (p. 23). Note that the distances quoted in the gazetteer apply to roads and, when planning your journey, it is important to allow for any ferry crossings involved, especially in the fjord areas.

EASTERN NORWAY

The southern part of Norway falls naturally into two regions and this section deals with the long, deep eastern valleys that drop down from the central plateaus to the Skagerrak and Oslofjord. One of the most northerly valleys, Gudbrandsdalen, provides the main link between Oslo and Trondheim and thence northern Norway. Several others, notably Hallingdal and

Setesdal, offer throughways to the western fjords of our next section.

These valleys harbour Norway's most famous winter sports resorts, and reach to the fringes of some of its most magnificent hiking country – Hardangervidda, Jotunheimen, Dovrefjell. The region also includes two major inland waterway systems: Mjøsa, the country's largest lake, and the Telemark Canal probing deep into the mountains. It was in Telemark and in Hallingdal that the art of rose painting achieved its finest expression and in these areas, too, that some of the best examples of early stave churches survive. Telemark is also known as the home of modern skiing.

Despite the ravages of fire and battle, much attractive rural and urban architecture survives. There are interesting contrasts between the weathered old homesteads of the mountain valleys or coastal fishing villages, and the bright white-painted houses which proliferated along the coast when white paint (more expensive than the rest) became a status symbol and mark of affluence. These coastal waters, incidentally, are said to be the warmest north of the Mediterranean. The imprint of the Danish-Norwegian king, Christian IV, is apparent, too, in townships ranging from Oslo to Røros, based on the Renaissance grid plan principle which reduced the hazard of fire.

Dombås   E8

(pop. 1200) This is a winter sports resort and centre for the Dovrefjell region. It stands at the junction of roads for Oslo, Trondheim and Ålesund. At **Dovre** (13km/8mi S), Tofte farm illustrates Viking Age traditions. From **Fokstua** (10km/6mi N) there are splendid views of Snøhetta (2286m/7500ft) and access to Fokstumyra moors, famous for their flora and fauna. *Oslo 345km/214mi.*

Fagernes   H8

(pop. 2500) This is the small urban hub of the Valdres valley as it bores its way north west towards the mountain massif of Jotunheimen. It is also the terminus of the Valdres railway, which starts out from Oslo. Valdres Folk Museum has a good collection of ancient timber buildings and there are stave churches to be seen in or near the valley, such as those of **Reinli** and **Hedalen** (respectively about 25km/15mi and 60km/37mi SE) and **Lomen** (about 30km/18mi NW). From mountain hotels there are fine views of Jotunheimen, but the setting and the views become increasingly stunning as you climb north up the valley from Fagernes to **Beitostølen** (40km/25mi), a popu-

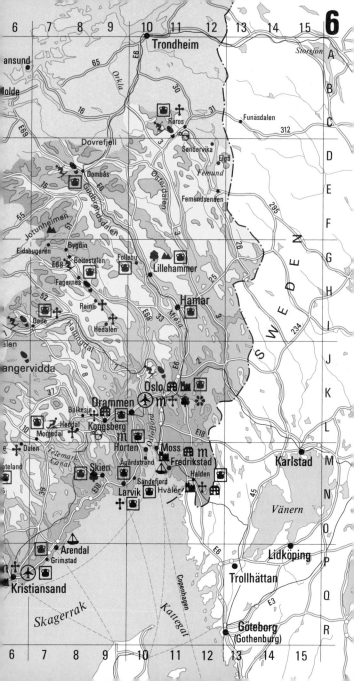

Jotunkeimen mountains

lar winter sports centre with special facilities for the handicapped, and **Bygdin** (53km/33mi) at the foot of Jotunheimen massif. Opportunities for hiking, climbing and fishing in the area are legion. From Bygdin, there is a high-altitude motorboat route westwards along Bygdin lake to **Eidsbugaren**. From Bygdin, too, begins the superb Jotunheimen Road running east across the mountain plateau to **Skåbu** (52km/32mi), a truly scenic throroughfare leading eventually to Gudbrandsdalen. Northwards from Bygdin, the main road reaches its highest point at Valdresflya (8km/5mi).
Bergen 348km/215mi.

Fredrikstad   N11

(pop. 30,000) One of Norway's showplaces is the old fortress town facing the newer districts of Fredrikstad (ferry link with Denmark) across the River Glomma. Within its walls are the beautifully preserved cobbled streets, houses, barracks, *etc*, of the fortified town founded and developed in the 17th and 18th centuries,

in which today many craftsmen and signers have made their studios where y can watch them at work. Outside the wa is a pinnacle topped by the slightly earl Kongsten Fort, popular for outings a festivals. West of Fredrikstad is famous sailing centre of **Hankø** and sou is the resort area of the **Hvaler islands**. the east the countryside is dotted with p historic remains, many of which can visited by taking the Road of the Ancier (highway 110) for 17km/10mi towar Skjeberg. Sights include burial moun Bronze Age rock carvings (**Begby, Horn** and **Solberg**) and the impressive sto circles of the 2000-year-old burial grou at **Hunn**. *Oslo 88km/54mi.*

Geilo

(pop. 2000) Scandinavia's best-known resort is spread beside one of a ser of small lakes in a shallow valley betwe the plateaus of Hardangervidda a Hallingskarvet. It has several chairlifts a drag lifts, 100km/62mi of marked ski tra and accommodation of all grades.

rdangervidda

mmer, it offers fine walking, fishing and
ling, and good excursions for motorists.
ol Museum (11km/7mi NE) illustrates a
rm complex from the 18th century; only
m/½mi further is 13th-century Hol
hurch. *Oslo 250km/155mi.*

Ialden N12

op. 27,000) This town is on the River
sta flowing into Iddefjord which forms
e border between Norway and Sweden.
oday bustling with timber and other
dustries, it was for long a strategic
tpost against Sweden and is dominated
the great fortress of Fredriksten, begun
1661, on the crags above the town. Its
mparts, towers and underground
assages are fascinating to visit, with
teresting museums and superb views.
alden's older buildings are in gracious
mpire style, including Immanuel
hurch, and Fredrikshalds Theatre has a
aroque stage, unique in Norway. Near
ie town is 18th-century Rød Manor and,
km/5mi W, the impressive **Svinesund**
ridge, over Iddefjord to Sweden, soars
gh above the regular excursion boats
at go to Strömstad in Sweden. *Oslo
9km/74mi.*

Iamar H11

op. 16,000) Hamar is a pleasant small
wn beside Mjøsa, Norway's largest lake.
y the ruins of its 12th-century cathedral
the Hedemark Museum with an open-
r folk collection, but a more famous
traction is the Railway Museum with its
ncient rolling stock still in operation.
lso notable is the *Skibladner*, launched in
856 and possibly the world's oldest
addle boat still functioning. It plies a
gular route across Mjøsa's waters be-
ween Eidsvoll, Hamar, Gjøvik and Lil-
hammer. *Oslo 123km/76mi.*

Hardangervidda K6

This rocky mountainous plateau, covering about 7500sq km/2900sq mi at an
average height of 1000–1250m/3300–
4000ft, offers magnificent trekking for the
experienced. It is broken up by innumerable lakes and pools and Norway's biggest
herds of wild reindeer roam its lonely
landscapes. To the north west, the plateau
descends abruptly to the western fjords
creating dramatic ravines, as can be seen
from the Geilo-Voss/Bergen road that
plunges into the narrow, tortuous valley of
Måbødalen to Eidfjord, an arm of
Hardangerfjord. At the head of this valley,
the thunderous waterfall of **Vøringfoss**
(visible from the grounds of a hotel) is
spectacular.

Horten M10

(pop. 14,000) The interesting Naval
Museum of Karl Johansvern reflects
Horten's original status as Norway's pre-
mier naval base (now Bergen). The town
is linked by regular ferry to Moss across
Oslofjord. In Borre Nature Park (3km/
2mi S) 29 great burial mounds include
those of the Ynglinge kings and queens
said to be descended from Odin himself.
Ågårdstrand (10km/6mi S) is a charming place of neat wooden houses and
flower-filled gardens. Its bridge was made
famous by Munch's painting *Girls on the
Bridge* (1899) and his humble home here is
a museum. *Oslo 90km/56mi.*

Hovden L5

The beautiful valley of Setesdal penetrates deep into the heart of the mountains and, near the head of it, is the
lakeside summer and winter sports centre
of Hovden. A distinctive peasant culture
has survived in this once remote valley,
silverware being one of many traditional

Stave church, Heddal

handicrafts. **Bykle** (29km/18mi S) is a typical Setesdal village, its church decorated with folk art. Near **Flateland** (50km/31mi S) is the excellent Setesdal open-air museum of Rygnestad. *Kristiansand 219km/136mi.*

Kongsberg   L9
(pop. 19,000) the town is attractively placed on the River Lågen with one of several waterfalls tumbling through the centre. It was founded by Christian IV in 1624 after the discovery of silver in the area. The silver mines at **Saggrenda** (7km/4mi S) which at their peak employed 4500 miners, closed in 1957, but visits are arranged throughout summer, travelling by the little mining train under the guidance of an old miner. In the town is the interesting Mining Museum and, near it, Norway's modern Royal Mint. Kongsberg's large Rococo church (1761) is most impressive. It can seat 2400 and the lavish decor gives it a theatrical appearance, complete with enclosed boxes from which visiting royalty and local dignitaries could gaze down upon the congregation. Though the interior is wood, it has been painted to resembl marble, and the final touch is added glittering locally-made candelabra. Lågd Museum is a collection of old farm buil ings illustrating peasant culture. A cl near the town bears the monograms every Norwegian king since 1623.

Kongsberg lies at a major crossroa of routes to south and west Norwa **Heddal** (46km/29mi SW) has the larg and grandest stave church in Norw (magnificent carvings), dating from t 13th century. **Bolkesjø** (27km/17mi V is a delightful small resort set in typic Telemark forested mountain scenery. *O 81km/50mi.*

Kristiansand   Q
(pop. 61,000) One of the many tow founded (1641) by Christian IV, Kristia sand is a bustling port and capital of t south coast. There are ferries to the U and Denmark. Shipping and exports a its principal activities, and there is a salt seafaring atmosphere about the city, and n

st round the fish market where live fish
: sold from troughs, and in the several
rbours bobbing with pleasure boats.
storically, the most interesting sights are
dieval Oddernes Church (runic stone in
: churchyard), Christiansholms Fort
74) bristling with old cannon, and Vest-
der open-air museum. There are lovely
at trips out through the skerries, and
m Grovane (20km/12mi NW) an 1895
am train, operated by the Setesdal Rail-
y Hobby Club, chugs along 5km/3mi of
ck through a delightful setting.
Grimstad (48km/30mi N) has a beauti-
position looking out to the skerries; it
s here that Ibsen served as an apoth-
ry's assistant when he wrote his first
ay, and the house where he lived is now a
seum. Prettily terraced against the hill-
es round its harbours, **Arendal** (67km/
mi N) is one of the popular seaside and
ating centres of this coast. Another
Mandal (42km/26mi S), Norway's
thernmost town with a famous sandy
ach (Sjøsander), 3km/2mi long. *Kristian-
d–Oslo 322km/200mi.*

arvik   **N9**
op. 8650) This small town on an inlet of
slofjord has regular ferry links with
ederikshavn, Denmark. Points of inter-
t include the church (1677), the Marine Museum in the old Customs House
d Herregården with the Larvik Museum.
e surroundings have much worth seeing.
the south there is Stavern where the old
val base, built in 1750, has a number of
otected buildings. In the vicinity, to
e south west, is 12th-century **Tanum
urch** and, to the south-east, **Kaupang**,
orway's oldest known Viking trading
ntre, has been excavated. To the north
st, towards Sandefjord, is the stone
rcle of **Istrehågan** and the rock carvings
Jåberg.
Sandefjord itself (18km/11mi NE; pop.
,000) has long lived off the sea, its mer-
ant and whaling fleets making it Norway's
ird largest shipping centre; it has ferry
ks with Strömstad in Sweden. The
haling Museum is particularly interest-
g; others are the Maritime and Town
useums. The sandy beaches and rocky
ves of this coastline make it a top resort
ea.
lo 129km/80mi.

illehammer   **H10**
op. 21,000) This tourist and industrial
ntre is the gateway to the 200km/124mi-
ng Gudbrandsdal valley, the age-old
ute between Trondheim (and the Atlantic)
d Oslo. The River Mesna tumbles
rough it, dropping into Norway's largest

lake, Mjøsa, with summer trips on the historic paddle boat *Skibladner* (p. 77). The
collections of the Maihaugen open-air
museum – the life's work of a dentist,
Anders Sandvig – are among the best
in Norway, with 120 buildings from
Gudbrandsdal set in a leafy park. The
Lillehammer Art Gallery is also excellent.
The town offers many facilities for outdoor
activities, including guided mountain
hikes. **Aulestad**, near Follebu (18km/11mi
NW), is the home of the national poet,
Nobel prize winner Bjørnstjerne Bjørnson,
a fervent campaigner for human rights.
Now a museum, it is exactly as when he
died (1910).
Oslo 185km/115mi.

Morgedal   **L7**
Here traditionally is the cradle of modern
skiing. Its pioneer was Sondre Norheim
who introduced the simple binding which
firmly attached ski to boot while still allow-
ing the necessary freedom of movement;
from this idea developed all the more intricate bindings of the modern ski. His cottage, Øvrebrø, is a museum in a beautiful
situation above the village. At **Bjåland
Museum** there are collections of skis and
polar equipment; this is named after Olav
Bjåland, a native of Morgedal who partici-
pated in some of Amundsen's polar expeditions.
Oslo 195km/121mi.

Oslo   **K10**
(pop. 470,000) The Norwegian capital,
clustered round the head of Oslofjord,
is probably the most spacious city in
the world, its metropolitan area of over
450,000sq km/173,000sq mi consisting of
75 per cent forest and farmland and 5 per
cent water. Its fine deep harbour probes
into the heart of the city and, from it, the
great cruise ships come and go, and also
the ferry services to UK, Danish and North
German ports. It is built on some of the
world's oldest rocks and man's earliest traces
are 3000-year-old rock carvings near the
Seamen's School on the southern outskirts
of the city. Later history is found in the
ruins of 11th-century St Hallvard Church
and other buildings in the Gamlebyen (old
town) district, off Bispegata, east of Oslo
Central Station (Oslo S). The town gained
much greater importance at the end of the
13th century with the building of massive
Akershus fortress which was completely
destroyed by fire in 1624. Christian IV
then supervised the planning of the new
city to the west of the old site and renamed
it Christiania. It reverted to its original
name in 1905 when Norway gained her
independence from Sweden.

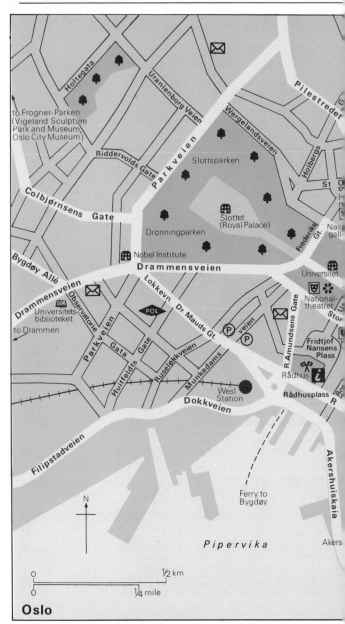

Oslo

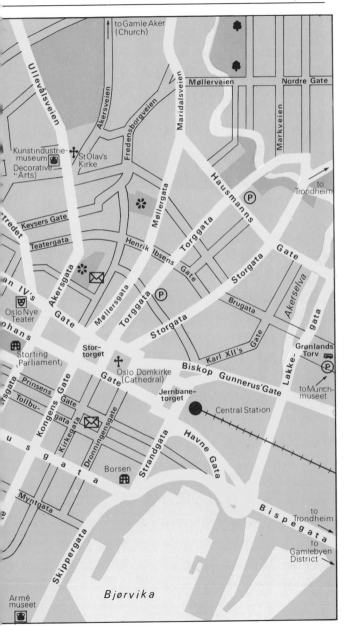

to Gamle Aker (Church)

Møllerveien

Nordre Gate

Markveien

Ullevålsveien

Akersveien

Fredensborgveien

Maridalsveien

Hausmanns

to Trondheim

Kunstindustrie-museum
Decorative "Arts"

St Olav's Kirke

Keysers Gate

Teatergata

Møllergata

Henrik Ibsens

Gate

Torggata

Storgata

Gate

Akerselva

gata

tredet

an IV's

Oslo Nye Teater

ohans

Storting (Parliament)

Akersgata

Gate

Møllersgata

Torggata

Stor-torget

Gate

Storgata

Brugata

Karl XII's Gate

Lakke-

Grønlands Torv

to Munch-museet

Oslo Domkirke (Cathedral)

Biskop Gunnerus'Gate

Jernbane-torget

gata

Prinsens

Gate

Kongens

Gate

Kirkegata

Dronningensgate

Tollbu-

u s g a t a

Myntgata

Borsen

Strandgata

Central Station

Havne Gata

Bispegata

to Trondheim

to Gamlebyen District

Skippergata

Armé museet

Bjørvika

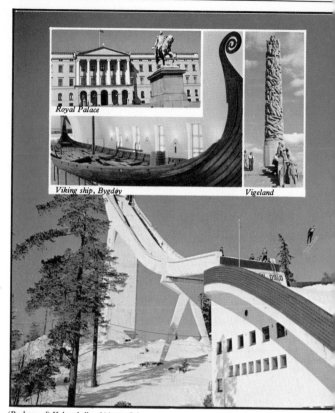

Royal Palace

Viking ship, Bygdøy

Vigeland

(Background) Holmenkollen ski jump, Oslo

Rising above Pipervika harbour on Rådhusplass (City Hall Square) is Oslo's famous City Hall, inaugurated in 1950 for the city's 900th anniversary and lavishly decorated in the 1930s and 40s. Huge murals illustrate many aspects of contemporary Norway (Sørensen, Rolfsen, Krohg). Using the harbourside entrance, you will find the Tourist Information Office (ask for the excellent *Oslo Guide* and a copy of *Oslo This Week*). From here regular sightseeing tours (various itineraries) leave. From here, too, come and go the commuter boats to and from outer Oslo, the sightseeing boats, the ferry across to Bygdøy (see below), and the daily shrimp boats with their catches fresh from the sea. Not far away a shipyard has been developed into the new cultural centre of Aker Brygge.

The Oslo Card (see Tourist Cards, 28) gives unlimited use of the ferries, buse subway and local trains that make up th city transport. Grønlands Torv, east of th newly rebuilt Oslo Central Station, is th main bus terminal. From the City Ha it is only a short walk north up Roa Amundsens gate to the National Theat and the parks that border Oslo's ma thoroughfare of Karl Johans gate, with th 19th-century Royal Palace (Changing the Guard daily at 1340) at one end an Oslo Central Station at the other. Th grounds of the Palace are open to all. Ea of the Parliament (*Storting*), the lower en of Karl Johans gate is a pedestrian shoppin precinct and, just off it, on Stortorget Oslo Cathedral built in 1694–9 (restore and with superb doors with fine bronz reliefs) and statue of Christian IV. A flower market flourishes on the square. Also on or just off this lively main street are the old university and Oslo's main shops.

Rising above the harbour, south of the City Hall, is the great hulk of Akershus Castle rebuilt in Renaissance style in the 17th century on the site of the medieval fortress; it houses the Defence and Resistance Museums, the latter a moving, factual memorial to World War II. If, however, you are attracted by seafaring adventures, you should head for **Bygdøy** (ferry from the City Hall). Here you will find the Viking Ships, the Kon-Tiki, Fram and Ra Museums and the Maritime Museum. The Viking Ships (*Oseberg*, *Gokstad* and *Tune*) are among the finest surviving. The *Fram* is the original vessel used for polar exploration by Nansen, Amundsen and Sverdrup from 1893–1912. Thor Heyerdahl's *Kon-Tiki*, the balsa raft he used for the voyage from Peru across the Pacific to Polynesia in 1947, has now been joined by his papyrus-built *Ra II* (replica of a vessel of ancient Egypt) in which his international expedition crossed the Atlantic in 1970. The Maritime Museum offers a splendid picture of seafaring Norway; outside is the polar exploration vessel *Gjøa* in which Amundsen was the first to negotiate the Northwest Passage. Near the Viking Ships is the Norwegian Folk Museum, a fine collection of ancient buildings including a 13th-century stave church, Lapland section and Henrik Ibsen's study.

Two other Oslo 'musts' focus on art. The Vigeland Sculpture Park and Museum in Frogner Park, north west of the centre, is dedicated to the imposing life's work of the remarkable sculptor Gustav Vigeland. His 192 sculpture groups in bronze, granite and wrought iron depict the various stages of the human cycle from birth to death. It culminates in a monolith illustrating the struggle for life and was completed in 1943, a year after his death. In the same park, 18th-century Frogner Manor contains the Oslo City Museum. North east of the centre is the Munch Museum devoted to Norway's foremost painter Edvard Munch whose often sombre but magnificent canvases reflect a childhood dominated by poverty, sickness and death. Nearby is the Natural History Museum with botanical gardens. To the north of the centre, the 12th-century church of Gamle Aker is worth seeking out. Other sights to be considered are the National Gallery and Historical Museum behind the old university.

On the heights behind the city is **Hol-** **menkollen** whose famous and huge ski jump is the scene of the annual Holmenkollen Ski Festival (March). Here is the Norwegian Ski Museum and the surroundings offer fine walks and views over the city. Another magnificent viewpoint is Tryvannstårnet observation tower at **Voksenkollen**. Both places can be reached by suburban train from the National Theatre, and a short walk. Northwards the mountains of the Nordmarka extend over an enormous area (splendid summer walking and winter skiing), dropping down to the west into the beautiful lake of Tyrifjord.

Oslo night life is fairly sedate and rather expensive, but there are plenty of good restaurants.

Røros   C11

(pop. 2000) Close by the Swedish border, this 17th-century mining town set on a high plateau has the dual attraction of its fine surroundings and an unusual industrial history. The town sprang up when copper working began in 1644 (discontinued in 1977), and much has been carefully preserved from those early days when Røros was linked by the Copper Way to the mining town of Falun in Sweden (p. 108), a way taken by many thousands in search of work or apprenticeships. Narrow streets, miners' cottages with turf roofs and blackened timbers, and more affluent houses in pastel tones can be seen. Conducted tours of the Christianus Quintus mine (8km/5mi) and the collections of the Copper Mine Museum, in the former administration building of Hyttstuggu, graphically illustrate mining conditions and the development of the town, which has provided the setting for many films as well as for the novels of Johan Falkberget (died 1967). The stone church dates from 1784. There are many marked hiking and skiing trails in the surroundings. *Oslo 401km/249mi.*

Skien   N9

(pop. 47,000) This industrial town was the birthplace of Henrik Ibsen. The small house to which the family moved in times of poverty, at Venstøp farm (5km/3mi NW), and the Ibsen house (Snipetorp) in the town centre can be visited; there is also a fine Ibsen collection in the Telemark County Museum in Søndre Brekke Park which also features many old houses from the region. From Skien, the **Telemark Canal**, built in 1892, penetrates the mountainous heart of the county to **Dalen** (130km/80mi W); it provides a memorable 9½-hour journey by regular passenger boat through many locks. *Oslo 139km/86mi.*

WESTERN FJORDS

This section covers the islands, fjords and communities of the west coast, an exception being Voss which lies in the valleys between Hardangerfjord and Sognefjord. It includes the ancient city of Bergen and the oil boom town of Stavanger. The sounds, bays, inlets and fjords of this coast offer some of the most breathtaking scenery anywhere in the world. Here rugged nature is at its most extravagant. Mountains rise sheer to great heights from the labyrinth of sea arms that probe far into the inland plateaus, sometimes close to the foot of great glaciers, among them Norway's largest, Jostedalsbreen. Yet, often the ruggedness is softened by the visible presence of man, and in particular by the hundreds of thousands of fruit trees that add soft mists of blossom in spring.

Villages and small towns cling to the edge of the fjords. The largest are closest to the sea, their quaysides lively with colourful, workmanlike activity drawn from the comings and goings of fishing and cargo vessels. Folk art and traditions are still active. Rose painting, originally imported from the eastern valleys, has developed in different styles, notably in the Hardangerfjord area. This area was also the original home of the *Hardingfele* (Hardanger fiddle) with its eight strings and haunting tones, which succeeded the bagpipes in the 16th century and has become a national instrument. Traditional weddings still occur, especially around midsummer at Voss. Throughout summer, the Fana folklore programme, near Bergen, gives a fine introduction to the region's past peasant culture.

An intensive network of passenger boat, ferry and hydrofoil services reaches scores of communities and, in turn, links with road or rail services with an impressive and almost invariable clockwork precision. Though organized excursions are arranged from main holiday centres, almost any journey on the public transport system qualifies as scenic sightseeing of a high order.

Ålesund   D5

(pop. 35,000) Built on three islands, this is a major fishing port and commercial centre, its quays bustling with the colourful workmanlike activities of fishing and cargo vessels, as well as the daily visits from the coastal service. From the top of Aksla, rising almost straight out of the town, there are magnificent views and, in the park at its feet, a statue to Gange Rolf, or Rollo, one of the colourful saga figures from this area, who became feudal lord of

Normandy and was ancestor of no less than William the Conqueror. The statue was a gift from the French town of Rouen. The Sunnmøre Museum (boats from the 7th century) and the Aquarium are interesting local sights.
Bergen 379km/235mi.

Bergen   K

(pop. 212,000) The approach to Bergen by sea is one of the most attractive in Europe. The city is ringed by steep mountains and the centre spreads out from the harbour in an architectural medley ranging from the medieval to the modern. Passenger ferries from the UK and Denmark, and the coastal vessels that leave almost daily for north Norway, berth on the north side of the harbour near Bergenhus fortress with 13th-century King Haakon's Hall and 16th-century Rosenkrantz Tower. Between here and the eastern head of the harbour is the imposing line of gabled houses from Hanseatic times. To the south side of the harbour come the hydrofoils and regular boats linking Bergen with many parts of the western fjords. Nearby, on the western headland is Nordnes parken and the Aquarium, northern Europe's largest and most modern. And at the head of the harbour is Torget where the daily open-air market of fish, fruit, vegetables, flowers and souvenirs bustles with activity all year round from 0830–1500. The fish stalls and troughs of live fish are special Bergen features.

The city was founded in 1070 by the Viking king Olav Kyrre and developed in the Middle Ages to become the capital of Norway and the largest port and trade centre of Scandinavia, a hub of Hanseatic power and wealth. Despite fires and other disasters, much still remains from those times. The Tourist Information Office on Torgalmenning, near the market, issues an excellent annual *Bergen Guide* (free

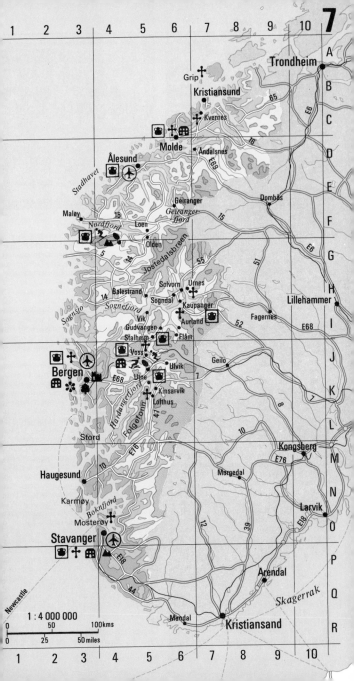

Ålesund

Bergen harbourside

detailing what's on, when and where, and it is also from here that many sightseeing excursions leave. If you prefer independent exploration, there is a 48-hour tourist ticket giving unlimited travel on public transport within the city.

Bergen's top attraction is undoubtedly Bryggen, the Hanseatic district on the north side of the harbour, where a row of ancient wooden houses with their high-pointed gables provides the frontage for a network of narrow alleys leading back into the courtyards, workshops and living quarters in which the employees of the Hansa merchants lived a virtually cloistered existence. Today it is an area of small workshops and restaurants where arts and crafts are still very much alive. In 1955, a section of Bryggen was destroyed by fire, but it has been partly reconstructed into a top-class hotel whose façade conforms in every detail with those of its ancient neighbours. Close to it is the new Bryggen Museum, displaying finds from excavations following the fire. Further east along the waterfront, one of the old houses is the Hanseatic Museum, its creaking stairs and original furnishings giving an excellent picture of the merchants' life style. Also in this part of town, behind Bryggen, is Maria Kirken (St Mary's Church), restored in the 19th century almost exactly to its original 12th-century condition (note the beautiful portals and superb 15th-century altar reredos).

If you follow Øvregaten eastwards from the church, you will soon come to the funicular station for Mount Fløien. Narrow alleys and steps wind and twist between the delightful old wooden houses stacked up the steep hillside of this district, well worth some footwork before you board the funicular. This whisks you up in a few minutes to Fløien (320m/1050ft) and a stunning aerial view

over the whole sprawl of the city. network of marked paths provides pler of opportunity for further exercise.

Returning to the Tourist Informati centre in Torgalmenning, you are withi short walk of several cultural sights in centre and south of the town. T Museum of Arts and Crafts and the Fis eries Museum (excellent displays illu trating the development of fishing ov the centuries) are only a brief stroll fro the small lake of Lille Lungegårdsvann whose south side are the Municipal Gallery, the Stenersen's Collection, a the Rasmus Meyer Collection (includi paintings by Munch) where piano recit are held on summer afternoons. Acr Lars Milles gate from here is the ultr modern Grieg Hall, a main hub Bergen's cultural life. A few blocks to t south is the complex housing the Hi torical, Maritime and Natural Histo Museums by the Botanical Gardens.

Within a few minutes drive of the ci are three major attractions: Gamle Berge (Old Bergen) open-air museum, a colle tion of 18th- and 19th-century houses an shops; Fantoft stave church from la Viking times; and Trollhaugen, Edva Grieg's home, preserved with all its Vi toriana. Another 'must' in the environs the cable-car trip up mount Ulriken fc more breathtaking views.

Highly popular is Fana Folklore, a ranged several times weekly in summe and consisting of an evening out in th Fana countryside with traditional foc and entertainment. The principal event i Bergen's calendar is the Bergen Inte national Festival (late May to early Jun featuring all aspects of the arts with top class performances. *Oslo 495km/307mi.*

Geirangerfjord   E

This is arguably the most scenic o

Geirangerfjord

Norway's many stunning fjords. It is regularly visited by cruise ships for the awesome spectacle of the mountains which drop in sheer rock cliffs to the fjord waters, their façades streaming with waterfalls with names like the Seven Sisters, the Suitor and the Bridal Veil. The resort of **Geiranger** has good tourist facilities and acts as the starting point for magnificent tours north to Romsdalsfjord (see Molde) and south to Nordfjord (p. 99). From the summit of Dalsnibba (1496m/4908ft), accessible by road, the views to the fjord and surrounding peaks are breathtaking. *Bergen 397km/246mi.*

Hardangerfjord   K5

This great fjord system south of Bergen has good road and rail links (from Granvin via Voss) to Bergen and Oslo, as well as year-round road connections via Telemark to eastern Norway and Oslo, and through Setesdal to Kristiansand and southern Norway. Its folklore is rich (this is the original home of the Norwegians' national instrument, the Hardanger fiddle) and colourful children's weddings are a feature of the summer programme. Orchards are one of the region's assets – about 250,000 fruit trees in all, creating magnificent mists of blossom in May. These fruit trees were brought in medieval times by Cistercian monks. To the east rises the grandeur of Hardangervidda (p. 77) while the white shoulders of Folgefonn glacier glint above Sørfjord, a southern arm of the fjord system.

Several ferries link many of the com-

Nordfjord

Aurlandsfjord

munities across the waters. **Lofthus** on Sørfjord is a delightful resort in the heart of a major fruit-growing area; it was a favourite spot of Edvard Grieg and you can see the hut in which he composed in the garden of the splendid Hotel Ullensvang. The local church dates from the 13th century. **Kinsarvik** and **Utne**, on opposite sides of the mouth of Sørfjord, are both pleasant, the latter featuring the Hardanger Folk Museum. Agatunet, a few miles south along Sørfjord, is a particularly well-preserved traditional farm complex (30–40 buildings), now a museum. **Ulvik**, on one of the innermost tributary fjords of the system, is another pleasant summer resort set in orchard and farm country. *Kinsarvik–Bergen 129km/80mi.*

Kristiansund　　　　　B7

(pop. 18,500) This major fishing port, built on three islands and linked by two modern bridges, is a colourful lively place, its long quays bustling with seafaring activities. It was almost entirely rebuilt following destruction by the Germans in 1940. Kristiansund is a port of call on the daily coastal service from Bergen and is linked by a beautiful road through the rugged Sunndal valley to the resort of Oppdal (164km/102mi SE) on the main rail and road routes from Oslo to Trondheim. A recommended excursion is to **Grip island**, about 3 hours north west by boat, where you will find a haunting solitude in a deserted fishing village (stave church) looking out to great seascapes. Here a community of several hundred somehow survived political and natural storms in the 17th and 18th centuries. Another excursion (south) is to **Kvernes** stave church by ferry to Bremsnes and 14km/8mi by road. *Bergen 513km/318mi.*

Molde　　　　　　　D

(pop. 20,000) This smiling spacio town, famous for its roses, has a mag ficent position overlooking islan studded Romsdalsfjord, backed by a pan rama of 87 peaks whose full splendour best seen from the hilltop viewpoint Varden, 10 minutes drive from tow Molde is a port of call on the daily coas service. It was briefly the capital of fr Norway when King Haakon and the go ernment sheltered here in 1940, at whi time it was heavily bombed. The resulta modernity is striking, especially the Tov Hall with its roof garden and the ey catching church (1957, Finn Bryn) wi its interior mosaics, reliefs and dazzli stained glass. Two excellent collectio are the Romsdal Museum (40 buildin from the Viking Age onwards) and t Fisheries Museum (in the form of a fis ing village) on the island of Hjertøya. T island is also a favourite bathing place. popular local excursion is to **Trollkyrk** (Troll Church), a marble grotto wi subterranean waterfall; it is reached t road to Sylteseter (30km/18mi N), then hours walk. Molde's annual jazz festival July has an international reputation.

The whole of this coast is intricate fragmented by fjords and sounds, offerin many fine excursions by boat (includii fishing trips) and bus. **Åndalsnes** (po 3000; 35km/21mi and two ferries SE) h a fabulous setting by inner Rom dalsfjord, backed by steep mountains. It the terminus for the Rauma railw which, together with a scenically supe road, passes between the soaring mou tains and thunderous waterfalls of t Romsdal valley to Gudbrandsdal (see Li lehammer, p. 79). Another famous rou is Trollstigen (the Troll's Path) whic twists away south from Åndalsnes, pa the Stigfoss falls, eventually to Valldal and Geiranger (p. 87). *Molde–Bergen 446km/ 276mi.*

Nordfjord F4

For nearly 100km/62mi, the long narrow cleft of this fjord probes deep into the Stryn mountains and towards the foot of Jostedalsbreen, Norway's largest glacier. Måløy at the entrance to the fjord is served by the regular coastal service from Bergen, and bus services link the whole area with Otta on the main rail route through Gudbrandsdal. At the head of the fjord sit the resorts of **Stryn, Loen** and **Olden**, each with its own valley and lake, the last two beneath tongues of the glacier. There is summer skiing in the area and various routes across the glacier which should not, however, be attempted without a qualified guide. The area has experienced avalanches and rockfalls of great magnitude; one of them, in 1936, caused a tidal wave in the lake of Loen in which 74 lives and several farms were lost.

The resorts have excellent facilities and offer splendid excursions by boat, on foot or by road through very grand scenery. Highly recommended is the circuit Nordfjord–Grotli–Geiranger–Hellesylt–Nordfjord (about 200km/120mi). At Sandane, at the head of the southern tributary of Gloppenfjord, is the Nordfjord Folk Museum. *Sandane–Bergen 254km/158mi.*

Sognefjord H4

This is the first major fjord system north of Bergen, its magnificent complex of tributary fjords thrusting crooked fingers deep into the rugged interior dominated by the Jotunheimen mountains to the east and the great white glint of Jostedalsbreen (glacier) to the north. The shorelines are softened by orchards and their mists of blossom in spring. Main roads from Bergen, via Voss, and from Oslo, via Gol, plunge down to the southern shores of the fjord system and are linked by several ferries to the highways for the north. Regular services by passenger boat and hydrofoil also link the area with Bergen. One of the most stunning ferry routes in all Norway is from Gudvangen (p. 90) through Nærøyfjord which, in places, is no more than 380m/1250ft wide beneath sheer mountains soaring to over 900m/3000ft, their flanks astream with waterfalls. Not surprisingly this is a popular port of call for cruise ships, whose presence often adds to the impressiveness of the scene. Ferries link communities such as Gudvangen (Nærøyfjord), Aurland and Flåm (Aurlandsfjord), Kaupanger, Lærdal, and Årdalstangen (Årdalsfjord). **Flåm** is also the railhead for a

branch line of the Oslo–Bergen railway, forming part of the highly scenic 'Norway in a Nutshell' circuit from Voss (p. 90). From **Aurland**, spectacular minor roads swoop and plunge over the mountains to Lærdal or to Hol in Hallingdal. From **Kaupanger** (stave church and Sogn folk museum) and **Sogndal**, on the north shore of the fjord system, there are fabulous routes through the Lustrafjord, Fortunsdal and Sognefjell areas. There is a particularly fine 12th-century stave church at **Urnes** on the east shore of Lustrafjord, reached by boat from Solvorn.

Further west, ferries link Vangsnes across Sognefjord with Hella, Dragsvik and **Balestrand** which has long been a famous small fjordside resort, very popular with the British and with artists. There has always been an inn here for centuries, for this was a resting place in the days when it took two weeks to reach Bergen. Gradually the inn developed into the splendid hotel that dominates the waterfront. It was a favourite haunt of Kaiser Wilhelm II whose visits, accompanied by a naval flotilla, caused a certain amount of suspicion among the neutral Norwegians in World War I. Nevertheless, so taken was he with the place that Wilhelm had two monuments built in the area, one of them, to the Viking king Bele, placed on some Viking burial mounds at Balestrand. He was also here when fire broke out in the resort, and rushed over to direct fire-fighting operations. From Balestrand, a beautiful road leads on towards the north, first winding steeply up Gaularfjell with magnificent views. There are also boat trips up remote, lovely Fjærlandsfjord at the foot of Jostedalsbreen (glacier). *Kaupanger–Bergen 172km/106mi.*

Stavanger O4

(pop. 88,000) Norway's main North Sea oil base and boom town is the capital of Rogaland county, poised on the threshold of the labyrinthine Ryfylke fjords that penetrate deep into this rugged coastline. From here radiates a complex network of boat and hydrofoil services, serving many fjordside communities and providing a short cut to the coast further north, including Bergen. Stavanger is an ancient city, its cathedral dating from the 12th century, when it was begun by Bishop Reinald of Winchester. British craftsmen were probably brought over for the building of this great church, originally in Anglo Norman style, though it was badly damaged by fire in 1272 and a new Gothic chancel was completed in 1300. In contrast with the broad streets of the newer town, the narrow cobbled lanes near the cathedral and harbour offer an attractive old-world atmosphere for shopping. Gamle Stavanger (Old Stavanger), above the west side of the harbour, is particularly charming with its white-painted 18th- and 19th-century houses. Other special points of interest in town are Ledål Museum, a mansion from 1800; the Stavanger Museum with its archaeological, historical, zoological and nautical collections, and the Stavanger Art Gallery.

A wide range of fjord trips include beautiful Lysefjord, with the chance to climb to the top of Prekestolen (the Pulpit), a dramatic rock cliff soaring about 550m/1800ft out of the fjord (reached by boat, bus and on foot). Fjord fishing trips are popular and Stavanger has an important International Sea Fishing Festival every August. Utstein Kloster (monastery) on the island of Mosterøy, north of Stavanger, has a beautifully preserved medieval cloister. A little outside the town, the reconstructed Iron Age farm at Ullandhaug can be visited. Newest attraction is the King's Park (20km/12mi S), a huge leisure park whose wide-ranging amenities include a mammoth size Gulliver. *Oslo 584km/362mi, Bergen 149km/92mi.*

Voss   J5

(pop. 6000) One of Norway's most popular tourist centres, Voss is situated by a lake on the famous Oslo–Bergen railway, about halfway between Sognefjord and Hardangerfjord. It is popular both as a skiing resort and an excellent centre for summer excursions into spectacular fjord country. Much of it was destroyed by bombing in 1940, so most of the buildings

are new with a few notable exceptions. One of these is the fine church, stone-built in early Gothic but with a wooden octagonal tower, originally dating from about 1270. The interior has much interesting Baroque and Renaissance detail.

On the outskirts is Finneloftet, one of Norway's oldest secular wooden buildings (about 1250), and on a hillside above the town is Mølstertunet, a splendid open-air museum consisting of two farms, with a total of 16 buildings, graphically illustrating their development since the late Middle Ages and the tough conditions endured by the farming folk. You can see the outhouses in which the girls of the families slept – in summer in storehouses and in winter above the cattle for warmth. The museum is full of intriguing details, such as the candle marked off to calculate time as it burned down. A cable car to Hangur restaurant and a chairlift on to Hangurstoppen (817m/2680ft) give easy access to fine views and good walking.

One of Voss's greatest attractions is the variety of excursions that can be made through truly superb landscapes. 'Norway in a Nutshell' is a full-day round trip which combines bus, boat and rail travel incorporating **Gudvangen** and **Flåm** (see Sognefjord). If time is short, go at least on the first leg by road to **Stalheim** (36km/22mi NE) where the hotel perched on a mountain shelf offers phenomenal views down to Naerøyfjord. Near the hotel is a collection of traditional farm buildings and artefacts. Voss offers plenty of scope for summer activities, including fishing and windsurfing on the lake. See also Hardangerfjord. *Bergen 125km/78mi.*

Stavanger flower market

NORTH NORWAY

This section covers the immensely long narrow stretch of country from the former capital of Trondheim in the south to the Soviet border via the North Cape, and includes the island groups of the Lofotens and Vesterålen. The area is characterized by a lot of dramatic and lonely scenery, and rather few inhabitants, the ratio decreasing with the latitude!

Traces of the oldest culture (up to about 7000 BC) yet discovered in Scandinavia were found in Finnmark, the northernmost province (the Komsa culture, near Alta). The Same (Lapp) people (see also p. 63, 118) are the oldest known inhabitants of the far north, the Norwegians gradually moving in to trade, fish and farm. A further influx of immigrants from northern Sweden and Finland, and farmers from south Norway occurred in the 18th and 19th centuries. Reindeer breeding is still an important source of livelihood for many of the 30,000 Same people, some of whom follow the herds up to the mountain plateaus in spring and back to the coast in autumn.

Many communities suffered considerable damage during World War II, either by bombing or, in the case of Finnmark, by the scorched-earth policy of the retreating German army in 1944. Most towns therefore are largely modern, though many also have a collection of historic buildings preserving the past.

Fishing continues to be the backbone of the far north's economy and the triangular drying racks are features of almost every coastal community, as are the pastel and warm tones of the houses against an often stark setting. Seafishing trips, with tackle provided, are available in many places. There is also superb angling (salmon, sea trout, migratory char, *etc*) but the strict local regulations should be checked.

Alta E13
(pop. 7500) Traces of Norway's oldest human occupation – the Komsa culture of up to about 8000 BC – were found on nearby Komsafjell. Also significant are the rock carvings, about 2000–3000 years old, which can be seen at nearby Hjemmeluft and Amtmannsnes. The town developed from the mainly Same community of Bossekop whose important spring and autumn markets attracted Norwegians and neighbouring Swedes and Finns. Its growth was boosted by the exploitation of copper in the mid 19th century (since abandoned), and the English church at Kåfjord is from those times. Today slate quarrying is the main

industry. Boat trips on the River Alta can be arranged. It is arguably the best salmon river in the world, leased by the Dukes of Roxburghe and Westminster until 1953, and since then by Americans. *Oslo 2010km/1256mi.*

Bodø J6
(pop. 30,000) This airy town on the regular coastal service is a main launching point for the magnificent Lofoten islands (see Svolvaer) whose jagged mountain wall can be seen to even better advantage from Rønvikfjell (restaurant), 3km/2mi from the town centre. There are also regular services to Vaerøy and Røst with their fabulous bird colonies. For instance, Røst archipelago, about 100km/62mi NW, numbers about 800 inhabitants and 4 million birds, notably huge colonies of puffin and kittiwake. Bodø's modern cathedral (1956) is strikingly light and spacious, and the Nordland County Museum presents an excellent picture of the region. Two recommended excursions are to the old trading post at Kjerringøy (39km/24mi and one ferry north) and Saltstraum, about 20km/12mi SE. The latter is a narrow channel through which a seething tide-race surges every six hours, a phenomenal sight. Shoals of fish follow in the wake of the natural bait sucked in by the ferment, making it a favourite spot for fishermen. *Oslo 1283km/797mi.*

Hammerfest C13
(pop. 7500) Hammerfest's two claims to fame are that it is the world's northernmost town (70°40′) and was the first in Europe to get electric light (1891). Fishing and sealing are main occupations and there are huge deep-freeze installations. The modern church is splendid, its entire east wall in glowing stained glass. The town hall is the home of the Royal and Ancient Society of Polar Bears, with a

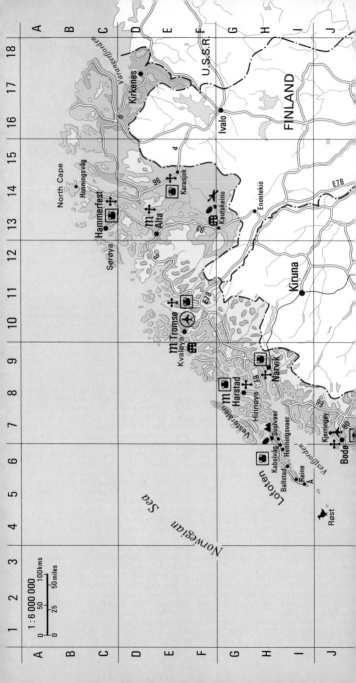

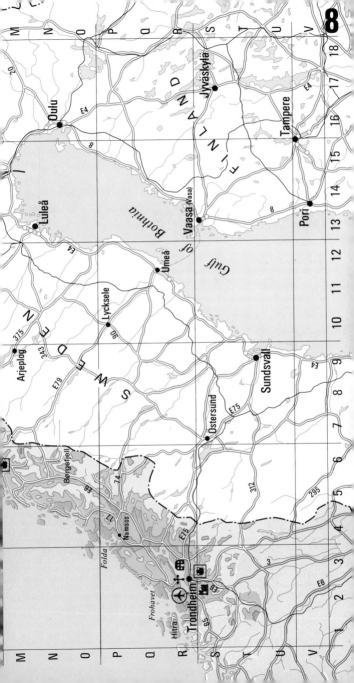

Svartisen, Mo i Rana

museum of Arctic trapping. The Meridian monument at Fuglenes commemorates the first international survey (1816–52) to determine the size and shape of the earth. Excursions include the North Cape. Hammerfest is on the regular coastal service. *Oslo 2154km/1338mi.*

Harstad   G8
(pop. 21,400) A port of call on the regular coastal service, this is a natural gateway to the Vesterålen and Lofoten island groups (see also Svolvaer) in grand surroundings. It is linked via the Tjeldsund road bridge to the mainland. At nearby Trondenes is the world's most northerly medieval church (1250), while that of Harstad is elegantly modern (1958). In the vicinity are the prehistoric rock paintings on Kjeøya islet and, at Grytøy, the Lundenes Bygdetun collection of farm buildings. The annual North Norway Music Festival is a major event around midsummer. *Oslo 1450km/900mi.*

Karasjok   E14
(pop. 1200) This village near the Finnish border is an important Same community. It has the only Lapp (Same) Museum in Norway and the world's largest library on Same subjects. The local high school has a permanent exhibition of Same handicrafts. The church (1810) is the oldest surviving in Finnmark. Excursions include river trips to a gold panning camp at **Storfossen** (60km/37mi SE). *Oslo 2276km/1414mi; Stockholm 1769km/1097mi.*

Kautokeino   G13
(pop. 1600) On a through road linking northern Norway and Finland, this is the

most important Same community in Finmark and its largest reindeer-breed parish. Many families still follow herds to the coastal grazing grounds e spring, returning in the autumn. Prio their departure, the Easter festival is highlight of the year, an occasion weddings in the modern church and sp ing events, with the brilliant Same c tumes much in evidence against the da ling snow. There are trips by reindeer sledding tours can be arranged in win while walking, canoeing and fishing summer pursuits. The Nord Sar Institute for research into Same affair based in Kautokeino. The traditional c of the silversmith is still very much al and workshops can be visited. *C 2124km/1320mi; Stockholm 1526k 946mi.*

Lofoten Islands see Svolvae

Mo i Rana   I
(pop. 10,000) A little south of the Arc Circle, Mo is a modern industrial cen on Ranafjord with a huge state-own iron foundry (guided tours available) a great factories. There are fine views fr Mofjell (410m/1345ft), reached by ca car, and an interesting collection of c farm buildings, Stenneset Bygdet (8km/5mi). To the north, the landscape dominated by Svartisen, Norway's seco largest glacier, to which excursions can arranged; another excursion north is the **Grønli** stalactite caves (22km/13m *Oslo 1035km/642mi.*

Narvik   H
(pop. 20,000) With some of the m modern port installations anywhe

...dnight sun, Lofoten Islands

...rvik is the world's biggest exporter of ...n ore, handling the huge output from ...e Swedish mines of Kiruna to which it is ...ked by railway. This extraordinary en-...eering feat was completed in 1902, and ...ries associated with the building of the ...ilway are part of the country's folklore. ...rvik was the object of intensive fighting ... World War II. There is a museum to ...e Battle of Narvik of 1940 and traces of ...avy German fortifications can still be ...en. The Peace Chapel commemorates ...sualties from both sides. The surround-...gs are imposing with snow-capped ...aks, including the Sleeping Queen (said ... resemble Queen Victoria on her ...athbed); for breathtaking views take the ...ble car to Fagernesfjell. Excursions in-...ude trips to the Lofotens (see Svolvaer). ...slo *1453km/902mi.*

North Cape   B14

...he towering granite cliffs soar out of the ...a to over 300m/1000ft forming Europe's ...orthernmost point (71°11'). The mid-...ght sun is visible, subject to weather, ...om 14 May to 30 July. The wild, bleak ...ateau is reached by road across Magerøy ...land from the fishing port of **Hon-...ngsvåg** (pop. 4600; 34km/21mi SE) on ...e regular coastal route. On the plateau is ...e North Cape Hall with restaurant and ...noramic views. Near Honningsvåg, a ...ame (Lapp) encampment can be visited ... fixed times. *Honningsvåg–Oslo 2170km/* ... *48mi.*

Svolvaer   H7

(pop. 4500) The 'capital' of the Lofoten islands has a setting of Alpine grandeur and is linked by boat to Bodø on the regular coastal service. The famous Lofoten Wall of mountains that rise to jagged peaks, almost sheer out of the sea, stretches for some 100km/62mi facing the mainland across Vestfjord. Since the Middle Ages the area has been the scene of extraordinary activity each year (usually February to April) because of the life cycle of the *skrei*, or mature cod, which means that it travels all the way from the Barents Sea to spawn in these waters. At this time, thousands of fishermen in hundreds of vessels (and it used to be many more) converge on the area for the famous Lofotens Fisheries. The sight against the dramatic backdrop of mountains, deeply shrouded in snow, is unforgettable. The Fisheries are controlled by their own 'government' which strictly regulates the zones and tackle permissible for different types of vessel and their catches; regulations are enforced by careful policing. The harvest of the sea is hung on the innumerable triangular drying racks used for stockfish, or handled by the many, sometimes pungent, fish-processing factories.

The east coast of the islands is punctuated by pretty fishing hamlets and villages such as **Kabelvåg** (Lofoten Museum and Aquarium), **Henningsvaer**, **Ballstad**, **Reine** and **Å**, clinging to

Arctic Cathedral, Tromsø

the shore beneath the mountains. With careful planning, you can go island-hopping, using regular bus and ferry routes. If you have a taste for the simple life, you can rent a *rørbu* (simple hut formerly used by fishermen), usually in a fantastic setting, but you will need to bring much of your own equipment. There are splendid walks and climbs, the latter including the famous Svolvaer 'Goat' (a rock formation in Fløyfjell above Svolvaer) with its two 'horns'; the intrepid jump from one to the other. Svolvaer and other Lofoten communities have long attracted many artists for whom there are special facilities. Among many excursions are boat trips to Trollfjord, perhaps the most awesome of all Norway's fjords.
Oslo 1387km/867mi.

Tromsø   E10
(pop. 45,000) Situated on an island in a narrow fjord and a port of call on the regular coastal service, this northern town is known as the 'capital' of north Norway because of its extensive industrial and educational activities. Fishing, sealing, whaling, the fur trade, shipping and allied industries are its main occupations. It was from Tromsø that Roald Amundsen, commemorated by a statue, set off on some of his polar expeditions, including his last ill-fated journey by seaplane in search of the

missing Italian, Umberto Nobile. And was from here that the king and gover ment left for five years exile in Britain, 1940. Here, too, is an important meteo logical station and the Northern Ligh Observatory.

Tromsø was one of the few northe towns that survived World War II u scathed and there are plenty of interesti old buildings, as well as the worl northernmost inn. Other points of intere are the Tromsø Museum (4km/2½mi SW including Same and regional collectio and Tromsø Town Museum. Tromsø Church (known as the Arctic Cathedr is a magnificent modern building design to harmonize with the surrounding pan rama. Tromsø Cathedral itself (1861) a large and simple wooden edifice. A cab car takes you up to Storsteinen (420 1378ft) and fabulous views. On neighbou ing Kvaløya island (road bridge) a 4000–5000-year-old rock carvings Skavberg farm (27km/17mi S) and histori buildings at Hella (28km/17mi S). O 1714km/1063mi.

Trondheim   R
(pop. 135,000) Originally called Nidar this was once the capital of Norway a its cultural, economic and religious hu founded by Olav Tryggvesson 997. It is port of call on the regular coastal servi

beautifully placed astride the looping
er Nid facing the fjord. The magni-
nt cathedral, scene of many coro-
ions, is a national shrine and the finest
thic edifice in northern Europe. It
ads on the burial place of Olav Har-
sson (Norway's patron saint) who was
n in the battle at Stiklestad
km/56mi N) in 1030, while seeking to
plete the Christianization of Norway.
e story of the battle is enacted each year
he end of July. Building of the cathed-
began in the early 12th century and
tinued until the 14th. English
dieval craftsmen were employed and
re are strong similarities to some
glish cathedrals, especially Lincoln.
er many ravages and plunderings, the
hedral was restored in 1869 (and sub-
uently) and is a truly impressive shrine
which soft grey-green soapstone con-
sts with shimmering stained glass, the
er the life's work of Gabriel Kielland.
ere are several sculptures by Gustav
geland. Next to the cathedral is the

12th-century Archbishop's residence.

The town was rebuilt following a disastrous fire in 1681 and the broad streets
and many houses and details date from
that time. Stiftsgården (1774), the Rococo
royal residence, is one of the largest
timber buildings in Europe. Along the
ancient wharves, rows of high-gabled
warehouses, many from the 17th century
and painted in rich colours, make a splendid impression. For fine general views of
the town, go to Kristiansten fortress (1682)
on a rocky eminence. Several major sights
are a little outside the town. Ringve
Manor, little changed since 1650, houses
the Tordenskjöld Museum and the ex-
ceptional Museum of Music, in which
many old and rare instruments can be seen
and heard, each room devoted to a different
period. The Trondheim Folk Museum at
Sverresborg has splendid collections.
Munkholmen island is a favourite excursion point where Viking executions
once took place and later a monastery was
built (no trace). *Oslo 545km/338mi.*

ccasin-seller, Trondheim

SWEDEN

Sweden's vital statistics alone are enough to fire the imagination of enthusiasts of wide open spaces. About 1600km/1000mi long by 390km/240mi wide, with 6400km/4000mi of coastline, 150,000 islands and 96,000 lakes, it carries a population of little more than 8¼ million. The impact of its landscapes falls somewhere between the hugeness of Finland's horizons and the ruggedness of Norway's heights, yet it has more streamlined and sophisticated amenities than either of its neighbours. Affluence is a tangible presence in Sweden, seen in smart properties, large cars, big and numerous motor cruisers, the proliferation of sleek trailers, big – sometimes huge – and well-stocked supermarkets, and in the considerable automation of many of its services.

Sweden's fluctuating fortunes have left their stamp on the countryside which vies with Denmark especially in the number of churches, castles and manor houses that punctuate the fertile southern farmlands. These southlands are in great contrast to the fells and forests, wild river valleys and immense lakescapes elsewhere. Like their neighbours, the Swedes escape into the countryside gratefully at every opportunity and they are well equipped to make the most of it, whatever their taste in outdoor activities. Long (and short) distance marked trails, canal and lake trips, canoeing routes and facilities for all levels of activity and budget help the visitor to follow suit.

Perhaps due to a sense of loss felt in the shift away from the simple priorities and culture bred by the wilderness, there is now a considerable movement to reaffirm traditions and to encourage or revive ancient crafts. Thus folk culture is still strong in many regions and enterprises devoted to *hemslöjd* (cottage industry) proliferate and range from regional organizations dedicated to maintaining high standards and researching forgotten skills to small workshops in the countryside, often set up by fugitives from city life.

For administrative purposes, Sweden is divided into 24 counties (*län*), but the names of the provinces – Dalarna, Skåne, Värmland, *etc*, – still survive.

SOUTH SWEDEN

The great blunt 'nose' of south Sweden separates the Baltic Sea from the Kattegat, nudging alongside the Danish islands so that it is not surprising that the southernmost beach-fringed province of Skåne remained politically part of Denmark until 1658. Thus many Skåne towns ⟨were⟩ founded by that energetic Danish ⟨king⟩ Christian IV, and the rich, rolling f⟨arm⟩lands of Skåne are dotted with prospe⟨rous⟩ farms and manors, and the castles bu⟨ilt to⟩ defend them. Iron Age mounds and V⟨iking⟩ Age runic stones are evidence of a m⟨uch⟩ earlier appreciation of this fruitful soil.

The Danes and Swedes fought long ⟨for⟩ this desirable piece of land, but there ⟨was⟩ less contest over the province of Små⟨land⟩ immediately to the north, characterize⟨d by⟩ rock, forests and lakes. It bred a pe⟨ople⟩ with a tough pioneer spirit who for⟨ged⟩ close-knit communities, and it was f⟨rom⟩ this region, and from the adjacent islan⟨d of⟩ Öland, that the greatest exodus of emig⟨rants⟩ took place in the depressed condition⟨s of⟩ the mid 19th century to exercise ⟨that⟩ pioneer spirit in the New World. ⟨The⟩ people of Småland are famous for ⟨the⟩ craftsmanship which still flourishes ⟨in⟩ workshops tucked away in the for⟨ests⟩ today. It remains, too, the leading re⟨gion⟩ for the production of fine glass.

Further out in the Baltic, the islan⟨d of⟩ Gotland had a brief medieval perio⟨d of⟩ glory as a hub of Hanseatic power. On ⟨the⟩ west coast, long before Gothenburg ⟨was⟩ founded to become Sweden's chief win⟨dow⟩ on the world, Bronze Age man impri⟨nted⟩ his remarkable rock carvings on ⟨the⟩ rugged terrain of Bohuslän to the no⟨rth.⟩ Overlapping into our central region, ⟨the⟩ construction of the Göta Canal in ⟨the⟩ century forged a new link between ⟨west⟩ and east across the great lakes of Vä⟨nern⟩ and Vättern. Also overlapping is ⟨a⟩ regular boat service through the contin⟨uous⟩ east coast archipelagoes, linking Ö⟨land⟩ island with Öregrund, north of Stockho⟨lm.⟩

Dalsland Canal

If you are an enthusiast of inland wa⟨ter⟩ways, you will find endless possibilitie⟨s⟩

intricate network of interlinked lakes
iced by the Dalsland Canal. The canal
54km/157mi long and rises by means of
locks to a total of 66m/216ft above its
ting point at **Köpmannebro** on Lake
ern; but it is better described as a
igable lake system since only about
m/6mi of its length is excavated canal.
e locks also give access to adjoining lakes
the area is a paradise for canoeists for
om there is an informative free booklet
English. Canoes and motor cruisers can
rented. There are passenger boat ser-
es in summer from Köpmannebro to
gtsfors, taking 6 hours. One of the
st interesting places along the route is
verud with its triple lock, aqueduct and
al museum. **Bengtsfors** is beautifully
ated, with a local culture museum. **Ed**,
the interlinked lake, Stora Lee, to the
t, is another charming centre. **Mellerud**
p. 3600), a pleasant small country town
Lake Vänern, is a main starting point
exploring the area. *Mellerud–Gothenburg
km/81mi.*

öta Canal F4

is remarkable waterway, created in the
h century, links the cities of **Gothenburg**
d Stockholm (and therefore the North
d Baltic Sea), an idyllic journey of
ee days by old-fashioned but quite com-
table motorships through rural south
eden. Only about one third of the total
518km/322mi is on artificial canals; the
t is through a chain of lakes and rivers,
luding Lakes Vänern and Vättern, a
ort stretch along the Baltic coast and the
al approach to Stockholm through Lake
ilaren. The vessels are raised by means
65 locks (to over 90m/300ft above sea
el and down again) including the im-
essive lock staircases at **Trollhättan** (p.
).

öteborg/Gothenburg H3

op. 500,000) Situated on the broad River
ota, this is Sweden's principal port and
ovides many visitors with their first
mpse of the country. It has sea links
th the UK and Denmark. It was founded
1621 by Gustavus Adolphus who called in
utch planners; their canals are one of the
tractions today. These and the city's
any green spaces (including lush
ädgårdsföreningen) contribute to the in-
mate small-town atmosphere of the
ntre, despite the major harbour and signs
industry all around. Canals wind right
rough the older part of town, and a
pular way of sightseeing is by the broad,
t-bottomed 'paddan' boats that ply their
ters. There are also boat trips round the
rbour and out to Elfsborg fortress built

in the 17th century to protect the harbour
entrance.

The Gothenburg Card (see p. 28) and
other tourist tickets give unlimited travel
on city transport, including the tramcars
which Gothenburgers chose to retain, but
you will best appreciate the narrow streets,
squares and shopping precincts of the old
districts on foot. Major buildings include
the so-called Fish Church housing the fish
and seafood market, Kronhuset (1643)
with the City Museum, Kronhusbodarna
whose restored boutiques and handicraft
workshops create a turn-of-the-century
atmosphere, and Antikhallarna (Scandinavia's largest antique market). Among
several excellent collections, the Maritime
Museum is dedicated to navigation, ship-
building and fishing, and the Röhsska
Museum to arts and crafts.

From the old town, broad fashion-
able Kungsportsavenyn, popularly
known as 'Avenyn', leads to the Art
Museum, Concert Hall, City Theatre and
Library clustered round Carl Milles'
massively muscular statue of Poseidon
in Götaplatsen. Gothenburg is also
famous for its sports facilities (the Scan-
dinavium is the biggest indoor arena
in Scandinavia), exhibition halls and,
above all, the splendid amusement park
Liseberg, its facilities for family fun,
cultural entertainment, spectacular shows
and gardens second only to those of
Copenhagen's Tivoli.

From Gothenburg, you have easy access
to the complete contrasts of the Swedish
west coast: rocky Bohuslän to the north
(see Lysekil) and sandy Halland to the
south (see Halmstad). See also Göta Canal.
Stockholm 483km/300mi

Gotland H18

(pop. 55,000) The island lies about 65km/
40mi east of the mainland to which it is
linked by regular air and sea services. It
is about 120km/75mi long by 56km/35mi
wide and is packed with interest: Bronze
Age stone heaps or great ship-shaped stone
burial settings, Iron Age fortresses, some
of the best extant runic, or picture, stones
and, above all, churches, fortifications and
houses from medieval times.

Gotland reached the height of its prosperity and fame in the 13th and 14th centuries when, for a while, Visby (pop.
20,000) – its capital on the west coast – was
one of the most powerful cities in the
Hanseatic League. Subsequently it alter-
nated between Danish and Swedish domination, finally becoming Swedish in 1645.
Impressive remains survive of Visby's
medieval walls, originally about 3km/2mi
long and punctuated by 44 towers. The

Bunge

Stora Karlsö

oldest section is the sea wall and Powder Tower, and the best view is from the north or north east. This delightful town, famous for its roses, is peppered with medieval churches, many of interest though all in ruins except for the cathedral (Sta Maria). The dramatic ruins of St Nicolaus are used for performances of the annual mystic pageant opera – *Petrus de Dacia* by Friedrich Mehler (early July-early August). It is a moving spectacle of very high standard, based on the life and writings of a 13th-century Dominican prior. Tall stepped-gable storehouses from Hanseatic times add to the medieval atmosphere; Gamla Apotek and other buildings along Strandgatan are also fine examples. The former Hanseatic harbour (Almedalen) is now a park. Gotland's Historical Museum (Fornsalen) is among the finest in Sweden (outstanding picture stones).

The island's jagged coastline is mainly steep and noted for its marine stacks, though there are excellent sandy beaches, for example, at **Tofta**, south of Visby, and **Sudersand** on Fårö. The interior consists largely of a rugged limestone plateau (*alvar*), reaching to 78m/255ft at **Lojsta**, on which you may see the attractive *russ* (half-wild ponies). There are many rare plants, including 35 species of orchid. Farming (especially livestock breeding), fishing, and the cement industry are main occupations. The northern part of Gotland, including Fårö, is a restricted area

though sites of tourist interest may visited by foreigners (check with the to ist office). Among other main sights **Romakloster** (12th-century rui monastery, central Gotland), the stalac caves of **Lummelunda** (north west), splendid open-air museum at **Bu** (north), and the islet of **Stora Kar** with its fantastic bird life (boat trips fr Klintehamn). There are no less than medieval churches, some, such as tha **Dalhem**, displaying beautiful stai glass.

Gotland has good sports facilities well as its own particular Gotlan sports, best seen during Stångaspele kind of Gotland Olympics (early July) **Stånga** in the south.

Halmstad

(pop. 44,500) This is the main town the Halland coast south of Gothenbu famous for the long sandy beaches wh have made it one of Sweden's most po lar holiday areas. As well as bathing, th are good facilities for all kinds of w. sports, several golf courses (the bes **Tylösand**), and family attractions suc Miniland on the outskirts of Halmstad is also an old town with a 17th-cent castle and city walls. Two smaller seas towns north of Halmstad are **Falkenb** and **Varberg**, both with attractive streets and timber houses. Falkenberg the River Ätran, is renowned for salmon fishing right in the town; near

nar Castle

glarp has a well-known vintage aircraft
car museum. Varberg has sea links
h Denmark.

åstad (36km/22mi S) is known as the
mbledon of Scandinavia', scene of
ior tennis championships for over a cen-
y. The Halland hinterland has many old
ntry churches and prehistoric remains.
henburg 145km/90mi.

elsingborg **O5**
p. 81,000) The town faces Helsingør in
nmark (p. 41) across the narrowest part
the Sound, and Denmark and Sweden
ght hard for control of it; the last battle
s in 1710. Today it is a major seaport
l commercial centre. A few miles north,
19th-century palace of **Sofiero** can be
ited. At Åstrop (20km/12mi N) Check-
nt Sweden on E4 is a well-equipped rest
a and information centre for all aspects
holiday travel.
henburg 229km/142mi.

nköping **H8**
p. 78,600) One of Sweden's oldest cities,
ely situated at the southern tip of Lake
ttern, this is the home of the match
dustry, with a Match Museum housed in
original factory. There is also a good
unty Museum. Mark Twain, who spent
ee months here, praised the fine sun-
s. **Eksjö** (50km/31mi E) is charming
h some of Sweden's best preserved
uses from the 17th century. To the
rth on the eastern shore of Vättern,
änna (39km/24mi) is a small pretty
vn founded by Count Per Brahe in the
h century and known for its pepper-
nt rock. It has an interesting museum
dicated to the Arctic explorer S.A.
dré, who perished after attempting to
over the North Pole by balloon. From
ruined castle of Brahehus, a little to the
rth, there are superb views over the lake
the long island of **Visingsö** (20 mins by
ry) where there are also a number of
rches and ruins from the time of Brahe.
Vättern's western shore, **Hjo** (64km/

40mi N) is a former spa with turn-of-the-
century elegance, and **Karlsborg** (98km/
60mi N) has a mighty 19th–20th-century
fortress with military museum by the Göta
Canal. **High Chaparral** (about 70km/43mi
S) is the fulfilment of an industrialist's
dream of a Wild West town, with all-
family appeal.
Stockholm 327km/204mi.

Kalmar **L13**
(pop. 32,000) Scene of the Kalmar Union
in 1397 (p. 9), this historic town is also
known as the 'capital' of Sweden's most
famous, glass-making district. The medieval castle, fortified and enlarged by
Gustavus Vasa in the 16th century, is a
splendid sight looking across to Öland
island (p. 106) to which Kalmar is linked
by Europe's longest bridge (6km/4mi).
After a devastating fire in 1647, Kalmar
was rebuilt a short distance from the castle
and is now a busy industrial port. Its
Baroque cathedral (by Tessin) and Town
Hall are from the late 17th century.
In the thickly forested hinterland you
will find some of the world's most famous
glass factories. Many of them may be
visited (free) and several have exhibitions
and shops. The art of glass-blowing was
introduced by a Venetian glass-blower in-
vited by Gustavus Vasa in the 1550s. The
oldest glassworks (1742) in Småland is
Kosta (64km/40mi NW); **Orrefors** (42km/
26mi NW) began as an ironworks even
earlier (1726) but switched to glass in
1898, and its displays of historic and
modern crystal are simply stunning.
Småland is also known for the staggering
numbers it contributed to the great emigra-
tion of land-starved country folk to North
America, from the 1850s. **Klasatorpet**, a
typical homestead from those times, can be
visited near **Långasjö** (67km/42mi SW).
The poignant story of the emigrants is the
theme of Vilhelm Moberg's best-selling
four-part novel *The Emigrants*. He was born
just outside **Växjö** (pop. 40,300; 111km/
69mi W), which is still in the glass making

country, where the House of Emigrants is a small but exceptionally good museum which also provides a research centre for Swedish North Americans in search of their roots. In the same building is the Småland's Museum with a fine section on the history of glass. *Stockholm 393km/ 244mi.*

Karlskrona   N12
(pop. 33,400) Founded in 1680 as a base for the Swedish navy, this bustling port, incorporating 33 islands, is still the fleet's headquarters. Timber-built Amiralitets-kyrkan (Admiralty Church) dates from those early days and there are picturesque old quarters. The city has a very famous Maritime Museum with a particularly fine collection of figureheads. The archipelago clustering offshore is Sweden's southern-most and there are ferries to several islands. Fine examples of rock carvings may be seen at Hästhallen and Möckleryd near **Torhamn** to the south east. *Stockholm 479km/297mi.*

Kolmården   D13
To the north east of Norrköping, Kolmår-dens Djurpark is one of the finest zoos in Europe, and probably the largest in area. You can travel by cable car over some of its varied topography which shelters a Safari Park in five sections, a Dolphin-arium and a Swedish farm of 50 years ago in action. One of the latest additions is a beautiful Ecumenical Church. *Stockholm 133km/82mi.*

Kristianstad   O8
(pop. 30,800) Built in 1614 as a strong-hold against Swedish attack at a time when the province of Skåne was Danish, Kristianstad is a pleasant town on the River Helge. The ramparts were torn down in the mid 19th century, but two gates (18th and 19th centuries) and some old barracks remain. There is a fine main square and a number of interesting 17th-and 18th-century buildings, one of which houses the local history museum. Another rather special collection is the Film Museum in Sweden's oldest film studio. Trefaldighetskyrkan (Trinity Church) is from the 17th century. On the Helge river estuary (21km/13mi SE), **Åhus** lost its importance with the building of Kris-tianstad. This charming small town de-veloped round the great medieval castle (Aosehus), now in ruins by the habour. In Kungstugan, one of the many half-timbered houses which cluster round 13th-century Sta Maria church, the Swedish king Charles XI took refuge from the Danes in the 1670s. Åhus is a main centre for eel fishing, and smoked eel is a particular local delicacy. *Stock 546km/338mi.*

Linköping |
(pop. 41,300) This is a most attra town whose old district (Gamla Lin ing) is a cultural reservation of 17th–1 century houses of great charm. Her summer, you can see craftsmen wor in wood, clay or metal, and there is a s garden in which 200 spice and medi plants flourish. The cathedral is from mid 13th century with Romanesque Gothic features. Several notable 1 century churches in the surrounding clude Kaga Kyrka with frescoes and gant slim tower. *Stockholm 204km/12*

Lund
(pop. 42,100) This is one of Scandina most beautiful and fascinating c 19km/11mi NE of Malmö. It was four by Knud (Canute) in 1020 and bec Scandinavia's religious, political, cul and commercial centre in the Mi Ages. The cathedral (1145) is the fi Romanesque building in nortr

Lund Cathedral

Europe; its principal features include 14th-century astronomic clock, 15 century altarpiece, finely carved c stalls and an impressive mosaic of Ch in the apse. Adjoining it is Lundag park where the 16th-century red-b royal residence became the unive (founded 1666) and still serves as

ck carvings near Tanumshede

nexe to the present university (1882). ere are many winding old streets such charming Adelgatan, and in Kulturhis- iska Museet (called Kulturen) a splen- d collection of old farms and manors re- eates the past. The lively old-style irket is held in Mårtenstorget; in a rner of the square, the stepped-gable h-century Krognohuset contrasts ikingly with ultramodern Lunds onsthall art gallery. In the surrounding untryside are many traces of the past m Iron Age mounds to medieval urches, the latter including Dalby urch (1060). *Gothenburg 283km/175mi.*

ysekil   E2
op. 7800) This resort, about halfway tween Gothenburg and the Norwegian rder, is a main centre on the Bohuslän ast, a superb stretch of rocky shore and erries whose smooth pinkish granite, ich of it heather-covered, makes an sthetic setting for bathing, sailing, wind- rfing, skin diving, fishing or simply ing. Lysekil has excellent facilities for these activities. To the south, the

labyrinthine coastal waters embrace island systems such as Orust-Tjörn, linked by soaring and dramatic road bridges to **Stenungsund** on the mainland. A string of colourful fishing communities nestle among the coves and headlands, including **Smögen** and **Kungshamn**, north of Lysekil, where you can watch the fishing fleets come and go and attend lively fish auctions. Most have small hotels or self-catering cottages.

Strömstad (pop. 4700; 95km/59mi N), close to the Norwegian border, is another attractive and lively small town clustered round its fishing and passenger harbours from which there are boat trips to **Koster islands** and to **Halden** (p. 77) in Norway. A major feature of this area are the Bronze Age rock carvings, scores of which are scattered about the countryside. The small town of **Tanumshede** is the best placed for many of them; the most important are those of nearby Vitlycke. They depict ships, animals, hunting scenes, sunworshipping and many foot-prints thought to be connected with some death cult. *Gothenburg 141km/87mi.*

Malmö   Q5

(pop. 235,000) Sweden's third largest city is linked by hydrofoil and ferries to Copenhagen across Öresund. Malmö still has many lovely old buildings from the 16th–19th centuries; Lilla Torg is a particularly attractive square. A network of canals winds through the city and you can travel on them by sightseeing boat. The most interesting church is 14th-century St Petri kyrka (St Peter's) in Baltic Gothic style. Malmöhus Castle is a museum complex housing art, archaeological and historical collections. Among other museums are the Technical and Maritime Museums and the Carriage Museum (vehicles from the 18th century onwards). Some of Scandinavia's oldest monuments are to be seen in the surroundings (see Lund). *Gothenburg 290km/180mi.*

Mariestad   D8

(pop. 17,200) This small, pretty town of old timber houses is about halfway along the eastern shore of Lake Vänern. The whole countryside is dotted with prehistoric remains, rock carvings, burial mounds and medieval churches. The medieval church of **Södra Råda**, near Gullspång (38km/24mi N), is particularly notable. It has fabulous 14th-century murals. *Stockholm 306km/190mi.*

Midsummer Festival, Öland

Öland   L14

(pop. 23,000) Though not pretty in the conventional sense, this long thin island, 140km/87mi by 16km/10mi, is infinitely

fascinating. It is linked to Kalmar (p. 1 on the mainland by Europe's longest bri (6km/4mi). Some of the most interest traces of Scandinavia's earliest inhabita are to be seen here. Bronze and Iron A burial mounds and gravefields pepper whole island and there are many Vik runic stones and graves. The most sp tacular gravefield is that of **Gettlinge** in south west. At the important archaeolo cal site of **Eketorp** in the south east, a Viking ring-fort and a later medieval set ment have been reconstructed, us original building methods. The m community took the best land. Typi pretty little town on the west coast (fe link to Bornholm, Denmark), near a m sive four-square castle built by Gusta Vasa on an earlier foundation.

Agriculture has always been the islan principal mainstay, though in earlier tim the farming folk were given a hard time raiding Danes and the greed of Swed kings who took the best land. Typi features of Öland are its windmills (ab 400) and the communities of enclo farms which stand in a row cheek-by-jo often with a huddle of craftsmen's cotta nearby. The pattern is well illustrated the **Himmelsberga** cultural muse (Hembygdsmuseum) near the centre of island. Nearby at **Ismantorp** are the pressive remains of an Iron Age fort. several beautiful medieval churches, one the best preserved is at **Gärdslösa**, a li to the north.

The southern half of the island is v largely composed of a flat limestone pl (*alvar*), unique in Europe. It harbours r plants, including many normally fou in Siberia, the Alps or eastern Euro among them 30 species of orchid and of violet. On the island's southern **Ottenby** bird station monitors consid able ornithological activity. The centre the island has extensive deciduous fores and the north has areas of *alvar* a pinewoods.

Trollhättan

(pop. 42,500) The town lies near the ju tion of the canalized River Göta and La Vänern, where the total gradient about 44m/144ft is negotiated by locks, four of them in Trollhättan. H dreds of thousands of visitors come an ally to watch the cargo and passen boats passing through the lock staira The present locks were built in 1961, t two earlier systems dating from 18 and 1844 can be reached by pleasant fo paths. The water forces, trapped a used for power generation by giant pow stations, are released on a few of in July.

...stle and harbour, Vadstena

Lidköping (72km/45mi NE), on one of ...nern's southern inlets, is the home of ...rstrand, Sweden's most prestigious por-...lain factory, founded in 1726; it can be ...sited. The town's distinctive 17th-century ...d Council House was originally a hunt-...g pavilion. On a peninsula, 22km/13mi ...rth, lakeside **Läckö Castle** is a truly ...pressive Baroque pile, though of much ...rlier origins. At **Skara** (about 15km/9mi ...) is Sommarland, one of Scandinavia's ...ggest adventure parks (see p. 24). ...ockholm 430km/267mi.

...adstena   **E10**

...n a bay on Lake Vättern's eastern shore, ...is small town is a port of call on the Göta ...nal route and has a number of fine old ...ildings, including Klosterkyrkan (the ...lue Church'), an impressive limestone ...urch from the early 15th century with ...h interior and medieval wooden sculp-...res. The town is famous for its lace. The ...stle was founded by Gustavus Vasa in ...45. At **Rök** (30km/18mi S), the inscrip-...ns on one of the finest runic stones (9th ...ntury) in Sweden continue to confound ...holars. *Stockholm 248km/154mi.*

Ystad   **R7**

(pop. 14,300) This important harbour, from which there are ferry services to the Danish island of Bornholm (p. 50) and Poland, is also one of the best-preserved medieval towns in Sweden. There are about 300 half-timbered houses from the 16th century onwards, the oldest being Pilgrändsgården. Other notable buildings are Maria Church (built 13th century, enlarged in 15th), the well-preserved medieval Gråbrödrä (Grey Friars) monastery, and the Charlotte Berlins Museum, illustrating middle-class home life in the 19th century. At **Kåseberga** (19km/12mi SE), Scandinavia's largest ship-shaped stone circle (67m/220ft long) is a splendid relic of the Viking Age. A few miles east at **Backåra**, the old farm renovated by Dag Hammarskjöld is now a museum. The sand-fringed coastline is punctuated by attractive towns such as **Simrishamn** (39km/24mi NE), Sweden's second biggest fishing port with colour-washed houses, and picturesque **Kivik** (54km/33mi NE), a fruit-growing centre where a major traditional fair is held each summer. *Stockholm 618km/384mi.*

CENTRAL SWEDEN

This region stretches from the northern sections of the great lakes of Vänern and Vättern to the borders of Sweden's far north. It includes Stockholm and its archipelago, as well as the early cultural hubs of Sweden in the surroundings, notably the former capitals of Sigtuna and Uppsala. Much of the rest is often described as 'folkloric Sweden' and folk art, music, crafts, plays, customs and traditions are all very evident. This is particularly true of the region of Dalarna (especially round Lake Siljan), with its green hills, blue lakes, red cottages, white birches and Sweden's most southerly fell district rising to 1200m/3900ft. Midsummer celebrations round decorated maypoles are particularly lively in this area. Folk art lives on in the colourfully painted wooden Dalarna horses exported all over the world, and in the costumes still worn on festive occasions and the vivid decoration of furniture and walls in the attractive old wooden houses. The people of Dalarna were God-fearing folk and the scriptures provided recurring themes in their peasant art and plays. Minerals have been mined in the region since medieval times, notably from the famous copper mine of Falun. More recently the area has spawned the great iron and steel works so important to Dalarna's economy.

To the south west, the province of Värmland with its deep forests and fertile river valleys is also rich in folklore and is especially well organized for farmhouse and self-catering holidays. Hälsingland, too, bordering the Gulf of Bothnia, has several major folk gatherings.

Falun   G11
(pop. 30,100) This interesting capital of Dalarna has, since medieval times, been a major centre for copper mining. From early times was it linked by the 'Copper Way' with Røros in Norway (p. 83). Copper extraction reached its peak in the 17th century when it largely financed Sweden's part in the Thirty Years' War. After a devastating cave-in in 1687, declining production fell even further, but was later replaced by other minerals (especially iron) and chemicals, and these industries in due course expanded to other sites. Well worth visiting are the original mine and Stora Kopparbergs Museum which illustrates its history and the often grim conditions of the miners. The Dalarna Museum in Falun makes an excellent introduction to the culture of this colourful province, and Kristine Church in the main square is a fine 17th-century edifice. At **Sundborn**

(12km/7mi NE) the attractive home artist Carl Larsson can be visited. *Stockho 231km/143mi.*

Järvsö   B
(pop. 1500) This is the best-known res in the Ljusnan valley of Hälsingland, region rich in folklore. Traditional sk are kept alive at the handicraft centre Stenegården. A colourful home of Hälsingehambon, when about 2000 pa ticipants dance their way along the vall from **Kilafors** to Järvsö. **Delsbo**, by t wide Dellen lakes north east of Järvsö, another attractive centre with folk gathe ings. *Stockholm 336km/208mi.*

Karlstad   L
(pop. 51,200) This is the pleasant capital Värmland, a province known for its l erary associations (see also Sunne). A emigrant register and research facilities a maintained for Americans of Swedish de cent. Nearby **Alster** manor house, th gracious home of the great 19th-centu poet Gustaf Fröding, is a museum. Th town is well situated at the mouth of th river Klarälven where it flows into Lak Vänern. The Klarälven is one of Sweden longest, mightiest rivers and annually pr vides a highway for millions of floatin logs. At **Ransäter** (about 50km/31mi N the childhood home of poet Eric Gus Geijer is another museum. The rur museum in the same village is charmin and has an open-air theatre. But among th valley's most unusual attractions are th rafting holidays available on a 112km/70m river stretch. Participants collect all the equipment at **Edebäck** (about 40km/25m N of Ransäter) and are transported by bo to **Branäsäng** where, under supervision they build their own rafts from 9ft logs. The gentle, idyllic journey at the rive pace of about 1mph takes 5–7 days throug

ided hills and farmland back to Edebäck. mping equipment is provided. This ld be the fulfilment of a dream for any uld-be Huckleberry Finn. A few miles th of Edebäck the open-air museum of **rnåsen** is worth visiting. *Stockholm km/190mi.*

ebro **L10**
p. 88,000) The town is dominated by 14th-century castle and the mushroom- ped Svampen water (and view) tower, erunner of many imitators. Above all, it kes a good launching pad for a forested e-strewn area, which includes Sweden's est national park, Tiveden, between es Vänern and Vättern – excellent for h outdoor pursuits as hiking, canoeing d fishing. North of Örebro, the land- pes of Bergslagen are dotted with re- nders of the exploitation of the rich iron deposits found in the Middle Ages. Of cial interest is **Pershyttan**, near Nora out 30km/18mi N), where a marked il of 6km/4mi takes you past the old nes, furnaces, workers' houses and er paraphernalia of this ancient mining mmunity. Another 40km/25mi NE, the lage of **Grythyttan** is the attractive oduct of an 18th-century silver rush, th its old square, church and inn from ose times.
ockholm 196km/122mi.

jan **F9**
he lakes of Siljan and adjoining Orsasjön at the heart of a beautiful area of hills d woods, steeped in the traditions of folk lture and crafts for which Dalarna prov- e is famous. From viewpoints such as **leden** (near Leksand) reached by cable r, or **Gesundberget** (to the west of Siljan) ched by chairlift, you get a fine idea of e region. In summer regular boat ser- ces link several lakeside resorts. Here, b, the tradition of travelling to church by e distinctive long boats, reminiscent of king longships, is still maintained on mmer Sundays, especially in **Rättvik**, d church boat races are held amid much stivity, the main event being early in July om Västanvik to Leksand.
Principal resorts are Leksand, Hjortnäs, illberg, Rättvik, in the south, and Mora the north. **Leksand** (pop. 4200) is an ractive small town with a good number old timber houses from the 16th century wards. It was the home of Carl Hansson, e most representative of the Leksand hool of painters who drew inspiration om the scriptures and the life of the ople. The popular allegorical play *The oad to Heaven*, enacted in the open air at eksand every July, is a splendid example how God, the devil and sundry prophets

Dress from Leksland, Dalarna

and saints mingle in the affairs of Dalarna farming folk. There are many other plays of this kind in the region.

Leksand Church dates from the 13th century (rebuilt 1709–14) and has a 14th-century crucifix. A short distance north at **Hjortnäs** is the fascinating Tin Soldiers Museum. A little further north, in the small resort of **Tällberg**, the attractive home of painter Gustaf Ankacrona is a museum. **Rättvik** (pop. 4000) is also the home of a painter, Målar Erik Eliasson, the first of many to create the distinctive wall paintings of floral and biblical motifs, an art form which reached its peak in the early 19th century.

On the northern shore of Siljan, **Mora** (pop. 8800) has many associations with the great artist Anders Zorn and good museums illustrating his works, as well as peasant art and architecture. Hantverksbyn is a delightful district of shops and houses recently built in traditional style. Mora is the starting point for the marathon Wasaloppet (Wasa Race) every March, when 12,000 skiers follow the route tradi- tionally taken by Gustavus Vasa in the 16th century; it covers 85km/53mi to **Sälen** to the north west. **Våmhus** (15km/ 9mi N) retains the typical layout of grouped buildings where, in summer, you can watch such traditional crafts as basket- work and lacemaking from human hair. To the north, at **Fryksåsen**, an old summer farm can be seen in action in the hills above Orsasjön. **Nusnäs** (SE of Mora) is now the main source of

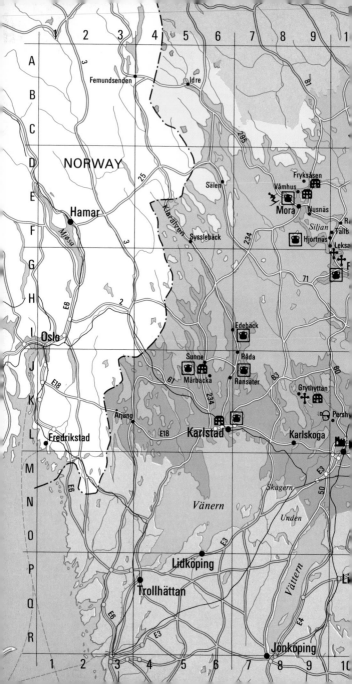

10

13 14 15 16 17 18 19 20 21 22

A
B
C
D
E
F
G
H
I
J
K
L
M
N
O
P
Q
R

Dellen
Hudiksvall
Delsbo

Gulf of Bothnia

Söderhamn

Kilafors

Sandviken Gävle

and

Gräsö
Oregrund

FINLAND

16

Åland Islands

Mariehamn
(Maarianhamina)

Helsinki

Sala Uppsala Björkö

m m

Skokloster

Västerås

Sigtuna Vallentuna m

Mälaren

Vaxholm

Strängnäs Stockholm Värmdö

Sandhamn

Eskilstuna

Gripsholm

E4

Baltic Sea

rköping

Utö

Copenhagen

Gotland

1 : 3 000 000
0   50kms
0   25miles

E4

E3

E4

16

I5

13 14 15 16 17 18 19 20 21 22

Dalarna wooden horses whose production dates back at least to 1840. *Rättvik–Stockholm 280km/175mi, Mora–Stockholm 319km/198mi.*

Stjärnsund   H12

This early 17th-century castle (4km/2½ mi S of Askersund) is one of Sweden's finest. It perches on a peninsula above the complex waterways that form the northern tip of Lake Vättern.
Stockholm 249km/154mi.

Stockholm   L16

(pop. 1,500,000) The city is magnificently placed on a series of islands and peninsulas at the point where the waters of the great inland lake system of Mälaren join the island-strewn Baltic sea. Modern ferries link it to the Åland islands and Finnish mainland ports. Stockholm is best experienced by boat or on foot combined with the extremely efficient public transport network. The city was traditionally founded by Birger Jarl who built a fortress here in 1252. Gustavus Vasa made it the capital of Sweden in 1523, and under Gustavus Adolphus it became the centre of an empire in the 17th century.

Sweden House on Hamngatan makes a good starting point, for here you find the Stockholm Tourist Association information centre with the latest details of what's on and where. The Stockholm Card (see Tourist Cards, p. 28) and other tourist cards give unlimited use of city buses and subway, the latter worth sampling in any case for the exotic decor of some of its stations (especially on the Blue Line). A season ticket also gives unlimited travel on the archipelago steamers. Sweden House is in the heart of the city with the main shopping and commercial area centred on Hamngatan, Sergels Torg and Hötorget. Sergels Torg, built on several levels, is dominated by the glassy modern building housing the Culture Centre (theatre, exhibitions, children's corner, foreign newspaper library). Sergels Torg is a traffic hub and converging point for underground shopping precincts, one of which leads to the Central Railway Station. Hötorget, with the big Concert Hall on one side, is the site of the bustling main open-air and covered markets. These two areas are more or less linked by Drottninggatan, a lively traffic-free shopping street.

Round the corner from Sweden House is Kungsträdgården, a park where there is always plenty going on in summer from folk and pop music to top classical concerts. The outdoor chess games here and in other city parks always attract interested onlookers. South of here, several bridges

lead to the Old Town (Gamla Stan) on an island. From these bridges you can watch fishermen trying their luck in the fast and amazingly clean waters of Strömmen linking Lake Mälaren with the Baltic; you can try your luck, too, but will need a permit (ask at Sweden House). Some bridges also cross the islet of Helgeandsholmen, largely occupied by the newly restored Riksdagshuset (Parliament). The Old Town is dominated by the massive 18th-century Royal Palace whose several museums include the beautifully arranged award-winning Royal Armoury. The nearby cathedral (Storkyrkan) was founded in the 13th century, reconstructed in 1736; its most remarkable treasure is the great sculpture in wood of St George and the dragon (1489). The Old Town is a maze of narrow traffic-free alleys full of antique and art shops, boutiques and restaurants. Its eastern waterfront, Skeppsbron, is lined with ancient merchant buildings and, in the south, the German Church (Tyskakyrkan) has a fine mid-17th-century interior.

The Old Town is also linked to the smaller islet of Riddarholmen where most of the kings of Sweden are buried in Riddarholm Church. From its west waterfront you look across Mälaren to one of Stockholm's most distinctive buildings, the City Hall (Stadshuset) built in 1923, setting for Nobel Prize ceremonies, with its piazzalike Blue Hall and majestic Golden Hall whose walls are entirely covered with 18 million glistening mosaic tiles depicting the history of Stockholm.

Sightseeing boats leave from several points with various itineraries through the city or to the islands, one of the most popular destinations being 17th-century Drottningholm Palace set in French-style parks, housing the exquisite court theatre (1764–6). There are regular performances here in summer, using the original stage machinery. Regular boats also provide links with Djurgården, a chunky peninsula with very varied attractions. The boats land near the museum housing the spectacular Royal Warship *Wasa*, which capsized on her maiden voyage in 1628 and was salvaged in 1961. It has been superbly preserved and restored and is one of the top sights of Stockholm. Beside it is the pleasure garden of Gröna Lunds Tivoli, smaller and less varied than Copenhagen's or Gothenburg's, but offering plenty of family fun in summer. Beyond is Skansen, the precursor of many similar open-air museums all over the world. Here you can see over 100 buildings from many parts of Sweden, as well as demonstrations of peasant skills. Next to it is the zoo. Two other museums in Djurgården are the

Drottningholm Palace

Background) Stockholm: old town and Lake Mälaren

Nordic Museum (showing the development of Scandinavia from the 16th century) and Prince Eugen's Waldemarsudde, his residence and art collections in lovely grounds. To the north of Djurgården is Kaknäs Tower, a fine viewpoint from the tallest building in Scandinavia (155m/508ft). Another unusual viewpoint, nearer the centre, is Katarinahissen (elevator) just south of the Old Town.

Stockholm is particularly rich in museums and has over 50 altogether: of special note are Gustavus III's Pavilion with its late 18th-century interiors, the Rosendal palace (*slott*) housing the memorabilia of the first king of the House of Bernadotte, the National Maritime Museum, and the Museum of Far Eastern Antiquities. One of the loveliest spots is north east of town at Lidingö where Millesgården, the home of the sculptor Carl Milles, is the waterside setting for his striking works, with marvellous views across to the city skyline.

Stockholm has plenty of fairly expensive night life. Many of its parks and historic buildings are used for concerts and other performances in the summer.

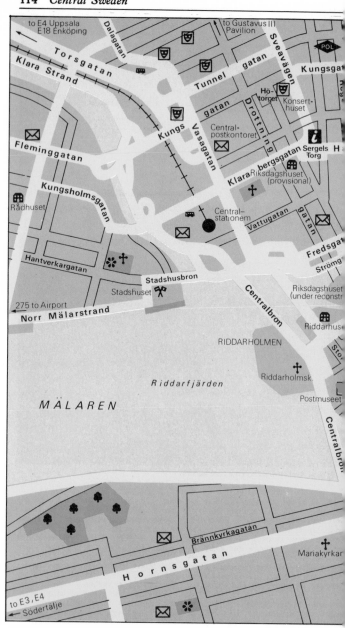

to E4 Uppsala
E18 Enköping

to Gustavus III
Pavilion

Dalagatan

Torsgatan

Klara Strand

Sveavägen

Kungsga

POL

Tunnel gatan

Hö-
torget

Konsert-
huset

Flemínggatan

Kungs

Vasagatan

gatan

Central-
postkontoret

Drottning

Klara

Riksbergsgatan

Sergels
Torg

H

Riksdagshuset
(provisional)

Kungsholmsgatan

Rådhuset

Central-
stationem

Vattugatan

gatan

Fredsga

Hantverkargatan

Strömg

Stadshusbron

Centralbron

Stadshuset

Riksdagshuset
(under reconstr

275 to Airport

Norr Mälarstrand

Riddarhus

RIDDARHOLMEN

Sto

Riddarfjärden

Riddarholmsk.

MÄLAREN

Postmuseet

Centralbro

Brännkyrkagatan

Mariakyrkar

Hornsgatan

to E3, E4
Södertälje

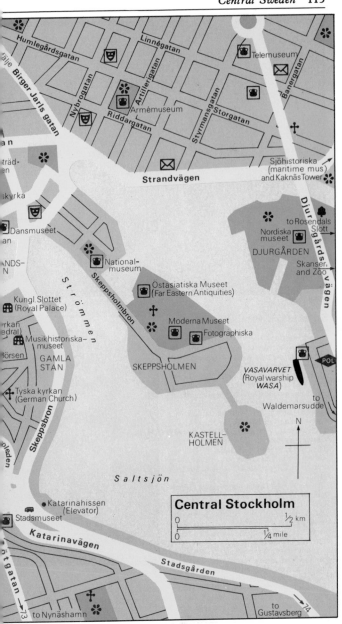

Humlegårdsgatan

Linnégatan

Telemuseum

Birger Jarls gatan

Nybrogatan

Artillerigatan

Riddargatan

Armémuseum

Styrmansgatan

Storgatan

Banérgatan

träd-
en

Strandvägen

Sjöhistoriska
(maritime mus.)
and Kaknäs Tower

skyrka

Dansmuseet

an

ANDS-
N

Nationalmuseum

Strömmen

Skeppsholmbron

to Rosendals
Slott

Nordiska
museet

Djurgårdsvägen

DJURGÅRDEN

Skanser
and Zoo

Kungl. Slottet
(Royal Palace)

Östasiatiska Museet
(Far Eastern Antiquities)

Moderna Museet

Fotographiska

rkan
edral)

Musikhistoriska-
museet

Börsen

GAMLA
STAN

SKEPPSHOLMEN

VASAVARVET
(Royal warship
WASA)

POL

Tyska kyrkan
(German Church)

to
Waldemarsudde

Skeppsbron

bleden

KASTELL-
HOLMEN

N

Saltsjön

Central Stockholm

0 — ½ km

0 — ¼ mile

Katarinahissen
(Elevator)

Stadsmuseet

Katarinavägen

Stadsgården

tgatan

to Nynäshamn

73

to
Gustavsberg

74

Gripsholm Castle

Stockholm Environs

Stockholm's beautiful archipelago extends for about 70km/43mi into the Baltic. The many attractive island destinations include sailing and bathing resorts, such as **Sandhamn** and **Utö**, or the townlet and museum fortress of **Vaxholm**. To the west and north are the many historic places by or near the Mälaren lake system, several of them accessible by excursion boat in summer. Westwards on the wooded island of **Björkö** are the traces of the 9th-century capital of Birka and many Viking graves. At Mariefred is 16th-century **Gripsholm Castle** with magnificent period interiors, an 18th-century theatre and Sweden's National Portrait Gallery.

Perhaps the most impressive destinations lie to the north of Stockholm. Here in the province of Uppland, about half of the 2000 runic stones in Scandinavia are to be found. A particularly interesting collection is in and beside the church of **Vallentuna**, only a short drive from the city. Lakeside **Sigtuna** (pop. 4800; 43km/26mi) succeeded Birka as capital and is Sweden's 'oldest' town – very pretty and colourful with a minute 18th-century town hall, 13th-century **Mariakyrka** (15th-century mural paintings) next to the medieval ruin of St Olof. A short drive away is **Skokloster**, one of

Skokloster

Sweden's most imposing castles, a majestic Baroque edifice with superb interiors 13th-century chapel and a vintage car museum.

...ke Mälaren

Undoubtedly, however, a major desti-
tion is **Uppsala** (pop. 101,800;
...km/42mi NW) one-time royal capital,
...t of the Archbishop of Sweden and site
...Scandinavia's oldest university (found-
...1477). The main monuments are
...ouped together on the slopes above the
...odern town. The two dominant ones are
...e great four-square red castle founded
...Gustavus Vasa in the 1540s, and the
...gant cathedral completed in 1435,
...here he and, traditionally, the relics of St
...ik are buried; it is the largest in Scandi-
...via. Don't miss the older and cosier
...oly Trinity Church almost next door.
...arious university buildings in the neigh-
...urhood include the great library, Caro-
...na Rediviva. Opposite the cathedral is
...e macabre but fascinating domed Ana-
...mical Theatre (1662) where public post-
...ortems were held in a steep-sided cir-
...lar auditorium. Carl von Linné, better
...nown as Linnaeus, the father of sys-
...matic botany, studied and taught in
...ppsala. His town and country homes are
...w museums. In Old Uppsala (3km/2mi
...), once the centre of heathen Sweden,
...u can see three great burial mounds of
...h-century Swedish kings and the flat
...ouncil Mound (Tingshögen) in a peace-
...l rural setting beside a 12th-century
...urch. This was formerly a cathedral and
...vice its present size, but despite the
...vages of fire and later additions and

changes, it is still a charming building.
Sala (pop. 11,200; 65km/40mi W of Uppsala) is a historic silver-mining centre; one
of the mines can be visited in summer.

Rottneros Manor

Sunne   J6

(pop. 4300) Three long lakes are interlinked along the very lovely Fryksdalen
valley where landscapes become wilder as
you travel north. Sunne is situated between two lakes and well placed for exploring the countryside so deeply associated with Sweden's most famous
writer Selma Lagerlöf. Her home at
Mårbacka is a much visited museum,
and many buildings in the area are known
both by their true names and by those
used in her novels. One of them is beautiful lakeside Rottneros Manor (her
'Ekeby'), its grounds graced by a hundred
fine sculptures. *Stockholm 367km/228mi.*

NORTH SWEDEN

From the mountainous spine of Scandinavia, scores of valleys rib the landscapes and link innumerable lakes on their way to the gulf of Bothnia. Most of the big inland provinces of Jämtland and Lappland are made up of superb, rugged wilderness territory, much of it protected as national parks with a host of outdoor activities, especially hiking, canoeing, white water rafting and fishing. The region includes Sweden's highest mountain Kebnekaise (2123m/6965ft). Though many of the marked trails require no more than normal fitness and proper equipment, others go through rough, difficult terrain and should not be attempted alone. Guided walks and courses are arranged by the Swedish Touring Club (STF), address on p. 29.

Most of Sweden's 15,000 Same (Lapp) citizens live in this region (see also pp. 63, 91) and though the majority now follow more conventional occupations, about 2500 still live entirely or in part from reindeer breeding, a few following the herds for long distances from winter pastures in the lowlands to summer grazing grounds in the mountains. Since 1971, reindeer breeding has been reserved by law for the Same people. Church festivals and winter fairs are big events attended by those from widely scattered communities.

The mountains are rich in minerals and attracted prospectors as early as the 17th century. The story can be followed in the museums and old sites in or near such mining towns as Kiruna and Arjeplog. The influence of mining and other commercial developments was not always beneficial to the local people and, as in other parts of the world, the introduction of hard liquor and different moral standards made their impact. So did the missionary zeal with which some Christian reformers set about obliterating the shamanist cult of the Same people, with its idols and magic drums. A notable example was the puritanical teaching spread by the Swedish priest Lars Levi Laestadius in the 19th century; this embodied a form of worship in which congregations were worked up into a trance-like frenzy that, to onlookers, must have seemed closer at times to the pagan than the Christian. The influence of Laestadianism was also very strong in parts of neighbouring Norwegian and Finnish Lapland. However, the Christian church in the north dates from much earlier times and there are some charming examples of primitive chapels, including some from the 17th century, on lonely islands and remote fells.

11

Abisko

This national park, with its Tourist statio covers 29sq km/11sq mi of wild count about 200km/120mi north of the Arc Circle. It is at the northern end of t King's Route (Kungsleden), a syste (430km/266mi) of marked trails that lea south along the mountainous spine Scandinavia to Ammarnäs, much of through spectacular scenery. On the way touches or gives access to several magni cent national parks – Stora Sjöfalle Sareks, Padjelanta – and Sweden's highe peak Kebnekaise (2123m/6965ft). It can joined from other points such as Saltoluok Tourist Station. You should seek local a vice about trails which can be attempte alone, and guided walks and course *Stockholm 1389km/863mi.*

Åre

Together with neighbouring **Duved**, th forms a lively resort area, the largest wi ter sports centre in Sweden, but al geared to a wide range of summer acti ities. A cable car takes you to the summ of Åreskutan (1320m/4330ft). Ask abo the low-priced Activity Pass which offe unlimited use of many local facilitie *Stockholm 665km/413mi.*

Arjeplog

(pop. 1800) This beautiful place is on t Silver Route from **Skellefteå** on the Gu of Bothnia into Norway. As early as th first half of the 17th century, silver ore w being mined at Nasafjäll, in the mountai 100km/62mi to the west, and the story told in the town's Silver Museum. Th 18th-century church has replaced or dating from those times. This is largely Same community and an important Wint Market takes place in early March. Th Silver Route also passes through **Arvidsja** (86km/53mi SE), another Same communi where both tents and many interestin

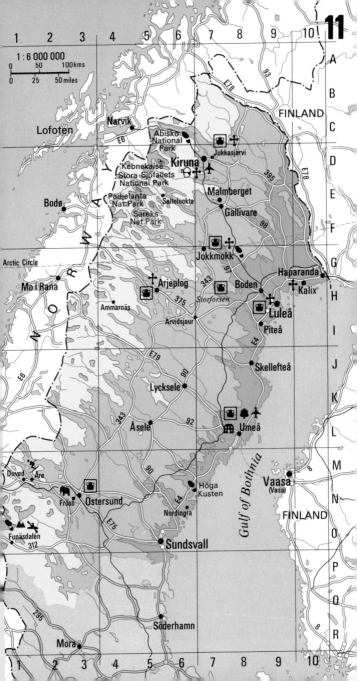

Abisko National Park

...rjeplog church

...uildings from the 18th century have been ...reserved. Reindeer roundups are held ...ere in June and July. *Stockholm ...51km/590mi.*

Funäsdalen O1

This is the main centre for Härjedalen, one of the country's most mountainous areas. The mountain ridges which form

Reindeer roundup

Altarpiece, Jukkasjärvi church

the spine of Scandinavia pass through here, with over a score of tops above 1000m/3280ft, the highest outside Lappland being Helag (1796m/5890ft). This is wilderness country, where elk, reindeer, wolverine, marten, otter, beaver and a handful of musk ox roam. Canoes can be rented and there is plenty of excellent fishing. Marked trails are classified according to difficulty and guides can be arranged. *Stockholm 560km/347mi.*

Jokkmokk   G7
(pop. 3200) Just north of the Arctic Circle, this small town serves several major hydroelectric power stations (visits arranged in summer). It is an important Same community, holding a major Winter Fair (early February), and its Arctic Circle Museum gives an excellent idea of Same life and history. The octagonal church is a replica of its 18th-century predecessor destroyed by fire. Muddus National Park, between Jokkmokk and Gällivare, is a splendid wilderness area with marked trails. *Stockholm 1073km/666mi.*

Kiruna   D7
(pop. 25,400) Iron was first exploited in this famous mining town when the railway was extended to Narvik (p. 94) in 1902. Daily mine tours are arranged. The church

(1902) whose style is inspired by Same tents, is decorated by notable artists of that period, including Prince Eugen. At **Jukkasjärvi** (22km/13mi E) a wooden church from the 17th-18th centuries has altar paintings by Bror Hjort depicting Laestadiansim (p. 118) and Same scenes. There is a homestead museum nearby. From here even the inexperienced can enjoy the thrills of shooting the rapids down the Torne river in rented canoes or rubber boats.
Stockholm 1287km/800mi.

Luleå   H
(pop. 42,200) This is the biggest town in Swedish Lapland, founded in 1621 at Gammelstad (10km/6mi N) whose 15th century church was later expanded and, together with its surrounding dwellings, forms the largest church town in the country – well worth a visit. In Luleå the regional Nordbotten Museum has the largest Same collections anywhere. **Piteå** (41km/25mi SW) is mainly industrial but with excellent beaches. Inland, the grandiose **Storforsen** (about 45km/28mi NW) are said to be Europe's biggest untamed rapids and waterfall (81m/265ft drop). There is an interesting Forestry Museum nearby. Northwards the road leads through **Kalix** with its 15th-century church to **Haparanda** which lies 127km/79mi

orforsen, River Pite

vay on the Finnish border at the outlet
the lovely Torneå valley. From here
ou can make boat trips into the Gulf
Bothnia's beautiful northernmost archi-
lago. *Stockholm 933km/579mi.*

stersund N3

op. 40,100) This natural gateway to the
mtland mountains is beautifully placed
the intricate shoreline of Lake Storsjön
d linked by bridge to **Frösö** (good zoo)
an island. The open-air museum of
mtli is interesting and there are lake trips
old steam boat. The lake is said to har-
ur a monster and in 1894 a company was
rmed to catch it! All attempts failed but
e equipment used is in the County
useum.
tockholm 572km/355mi.

undsvall O6

op. 55,300) This main commercial and
dustrial centre on the principal coastal
ghway that leads to northern Sweden
as largely rebuilt after a great fire in
888. Regular ferries link it across the Gulf
Bothnia with Vaasa, Finland (p. 62). It
also on the approach to the 'Steep Coast'
löga Kusten), the most dramatic section
Sweden's east coast, extending north
Sandö Bridge (91km/56mi N of
undsvall) for 65km/40mi to **Örnsköldsvik**.

Here the inland hills drop steeply to the sea,
sometimes forming sheer rocky cliffs, along
a twisted coastline of inlets and islands, its
wildness punctuated by fishing villages
and red farmsteads. The community of
Nordingrå is in the heart of the area and
Höga Kustenleden (Steep Coast Route) is a
marked hiking trail of about 130km/81mi.
Stockholm 386km/239mi.

Umeå L8
(pop. 50,000) The town is situated on the
River Umeå whose waters feed a whole
series of hydro-electric power stations and
provide a highway for millions of logs
annually. The town was rebuilt after a
great fire in 1888 and is famous for the
silver birches planted then, but typical old
buildings from the area are preserved in
the park of Gammlia, where you will also
find the County Museum. The timber-
sorting plant near the airport is an impressive sight and tours are arranged to
Stornorrfors, the giant hydro-electric
power station (15km/9mi W); a local phenomenon is the salmon jump (*laxhoppet*)
just below the dam. The area was the scene
of fierce fighting with the Russians in
1809; their headquarters in an 18th-century
manor house is preserved in Gammlia.
There is a regular service across the Gulf
of Bothnia to Vaasa, Finland (p. 62). *Stockholm
661km/410mi.*

INDEX

This index is in six separate parts. The first part (below) refers to all the general information in the book. Each of the five countries has its own index which refers to the gazetteer. In the last five indexes all the main entries are printed in heavy type. Map references are also printed in heavy type. The map page number precedes the grid reference.

DENMARK

FINLAND

ICELAND

ORWAY

SWEDEN